The
Luther
Journey

Herbert
Brokering

The Luther Journey

Thanks to Amy and Mark and the Apple computer for making production of this book possible.

Other Recent Books by Herbert Brokering
Pilgrimage to Luther's Germany
Pilgrimage to Renewal
Wholly Holy
Love Songs
Joy Songs

ISBN: 0-942562-02-X

Printed in the U.S.A.

Design: Robert Friederichsen
Cover photo by Mark Brokering

Brokering Press
11641 Palmer Road
Bloomington, MN 55437

Preface

In 1980, a small film crew followed and photographed Luther scholar Dr. Roland Bainton as he walked through many doors and on many roads where Luther once journeyed. Our efforts resulted in the film "Where Luther Walked." That time together inspired a recent book with Dr. Bainton: *Pilgrimage to Luther's Germany*, a photographic meditation on Luther's world.

For more than a decade Dr. Roland Bainton and I have gone into communities throughout the United States, Canada, and Japan, helping gatherings of all ages to transform Reformation and Renaissance facts into festivals. At the end of each festival we are always more aware of each other's worth, and of the primacy of Christ. Through celebrating the events in the life of Luther, we are introduced to Christ, and to one another. May this book do the same for those who use it.

Introduction

The pilgrimage journey of my ancestors began long ago in the land of Martin Luther. The shoes you see on the Brokering grave plaque pictured on the cover are but one pair of the many shoes that have walked the Luther journey. All who walk in those shoes are in some way heirs to that journey of faith.

In recent years I have found ways to be imaginative, creative, playful, childlike, and spiritual with historical data. History can be sung, prayed, visualized, photographed, danced, shaped, and dramatized. Facts are but one form of historical information. Facts always look for the warmth of the human being.

The Luther Journey explores the life and times of Martin Luther in several forms. Luther's life is presented here in a chronology, as a history story, as creative exercises, drama, and song. Three parallel columns guide you through your journey, with each column presenting another approach to history. A fourth column provides you with space to record your own thoughts and feelings, whether you are reading at home or taking an actual tour of Luther's land. This book will provide ways to internalize Luther's journey and to express your own journey.

The Luther Journey is for youth and adults. It is for those who are growing in faith. It is for the childlike who celebrate what they know and sing what they see and hear.

The Luther Journey is a textbook, tour book, workbook, storybook, music book, play book, and reference book. It is for the family, for confirmands, for special study groups, reformation committees, choirs, theater groups, and artists. The material provided is educational, inspirational, factual, artistic, and confessional.

How can this book be used? Read it aloud, sing it, use it as a basis for drama and reading theater, study it as a textbook, treat it as a workbook, use it as a diary or log. Consider it as a resource for the planning of Reformation festivals and programs.

Discover your own journey in Luther's journey. Use this book as an album, workbook, diary, log, or journal for recording thoughts and feelings. Fill it with ideas and emotions to share with others. Turn your journey into a journal.

While in Japan with Luther scholar Dr. Bainton, our journey took us into the home of the brilliant Christian artist Sadao Watanabe. He summed up his own life in these words: "Christian faith is artful. While it is to be studied, it is also to be imagined!"

The Luther Journey is for the mind, and it is also for the spirit.

Herbert Brokering

Contents

Luther Chronology

Luther History

1483

Hans and Margaretha Luder (Luther) move from Moehra in Thuringia, seventy miles northeast to Eisleben, a copper and slate mining area located at the foot of the Harz Mountains.

Moehra

Hans Luder (Luther) and Margaretha Ziegler were married in Moehra, a little farming town in Saxony, Germany. They then left the Luder farm and moved to Eisleben, eighty miles northeast of Moehra.

Hans and Margaretha lived during what is known as the Middle Ages, a time of castles, kings, knights, queens, dukes, power, peasants, beggars, death, and the Black Plague. There was much superstition in the beliefs of the people at this time.

In those days the Pope and the Emperor were often so close in power and alliances that economics, politics, faith, and law were as one.

The printing press was only thirty years old.

Columbus was just rigging his ships to sail.

Inventors were trying out new ideas. Copernicus was keenly watched and his findings about the earth were debated far and wide.

Many people felt discrimination. Some were tired of being trampled on and began reading old writings and seeing old paintings that made them feel important. They wanted to rebel.

Leonardo da Vinci was at work in Italy, painting. Michelangelo was flat on his back, painting the Sistine chapel in Rome.

Creative Exercises

At Moehra

Use your imagination when visiting Luther places or when reading the Luther story.

Ask why each town is important to Luther's history.

Know the chronology of Luther's life. A familiarity with the order of events will help you when visiting or reading about places in a nonchronological order.

Painting by Cranach of Hans Luder,
Martin's father

See faith from an historical perspective. Use Luther's history to put your own faith into perspective. Ask the questions: How is my own faith going on? What is the journey of my faith?

Look for the church life in Luther's Germany. Be open to discovering the church in different forms than you now know.

Become involved. Look, listen, feel, wonder, taste, hear, and understand. Ask about what you do not understand. Believe in the importance of discovering and discussing your feelings and insights with others in the group. Share your hope, trust, faith, needs, and resources.

Painting by Cranach of Margaretha Luder,
Martin's mother

Music was changing from plain song or Gregorian chant to new harmonies and melodies. The fourteenth century had used open octaves of fourths and fifths in most music. Musicians were just now beginning to use triads, playing in thirds.

Hans Luder would not stay long in Eisleben. He had his eye on a better life, beyond peasantry.

Margaretha was probably from a burgher family, professional citizens of Eisenach. She had a vision for her children that was fine and of faith.

Eisleben

November 10: Martin Luther, second child of Hans and Margaretha Luther, is born at Eisleben.

On November 10, 1483, around midnight, the second child was born to Margaretha and Hans Luder. The birth was by candlelight in the small mining village of Eisleben, in the rolling woods of the province of Saxony.

Sixty-two years later, after much travel and fame, this child would die in the same town, also in the night.

As with any newborn, there was no telling what its life was to be. When this child was out into the world, it would seem to many people that God had sent a prophet to be with them. Or an angel. So important would he grow up to be.

November 11: The infant is baptized in St. Peter-Paul Church, Eisleben, on St. Martin of Tours Day.

Leonardo da Vinci is painting "The Last Supper."

The next morning, on St. Martin's Day, the pious father Hans took his infant son to a fortress's baptism chapel. There he, a priest, and the child met for the baptism. This baptism would be a strong symbol of love and salvation in a stormy life to come. The sacrament of baptism was to Martin Luther an anchor of a boat tossed to and fro in a stormy sea.

In baptism the naked infant was often dipped into the water. This immersion was a sign of Christ's own death and resurrection given to the child. It was a picture of rebirth and salvation. It was a preview of a daily rebirth.

In later years the picture of daily renewal would be important to Martin. Kneeling and rising would become his own sign of death and resurrection. Through baptism he was immersed into the life of Christ.

Easter began to unfold in the tiny fortress room in St. Peter–Paul Church, Eisleben, when Martin was but one day old.

Learn to visualize along the way, whether reading or traveling.

Ask yourself how it must have felt to be Martin Luther when he was there. Ask how it feels so that you can make a connection between information and emotions.

Go through the journey from an emotional viewpoint.

At Eisleben

Think of origins, heritage, and family lineage.

Melanchton baptizing by Lucas Cranach

Talk about trusting God, and about how baptism is a base for that trust. Think of baptism as a way of life, a journey, a walk.

Create a Martin Luther party and celebrate each other.

Tell about your birthdays.

Have a mini-birthday party, even if it lasts only a few minutes.

Watch the time. At eleven P.M., think of Martin Luther's beginning at this time of night 500 years ago. Think of beginnings.

One should place before children and deeply impress upon them . . . common chief parts of faith, so that, having grasped them, they themselves could then read Scripture and confirm and fortify these articles the more and in this way become mighty in faith and Scripture. (Luther)

1484

Early summer: Hans and Margaretha Luther move to Mansfeld, village of miners and peddlers, surrounded by hills and overlooked by a majestic castle.

1486

Frederick the Wise becomes Duke of Saxony. He builds the Wittenburg Castle in northern Saxony. Maximilian I is crowned King of the Holy Roman Empire of the German Nation.

1488

March 12: Luther enters Mansfeld Latin school, near church, on St. George's Day, at the age of 4½ years.

1492

Alexander VI becomes Pope.

Columbus sets sail for the new world.

William Tyndale, England's great leader of Protestant reformation, is born.

1497

Near Easter: Luther goes to Cathedral School at Magdeburg, forty miles north of Mansfeld, and lives in the Order of the Common Brethren. He sees Prince William of Anhalt, now a beggar of the Franciscan order. Magdeburg is a commercial town on the Elbe River.

Mansfeld

When Martin was six months old, the family of three moved two miles west to Mansfeld. There Hans would supervise a silver mining company. He was a hard-working miner who wished for others a more pleasant life than that of the peasant. He felt the struggle of the common people and sympathized with their need to work so hard.

Both parents hoped their son Martin would one day be educated at a university, perhaps to study law. They did not wish for Martin to be trapped in the hard life of the peasant folk.

Sometimes they even imagined he would marry a rich lady, and with his education become a respectable leader somewhere in Saxony, Germany. And then too he would surely be able to care for his parents in their old age.

In later years, Martin remembered his father's hard work. Hans spoke up on behalf of workers and their rights. The Saxon son inherited his father's concern for the oppressed.

School was taught in Latin. For seven years, Martin learned his Latin grammar in the Mansfeld school. He began at age seven (some say at age four-and-a-half).

The games were also in Latin. Even the playground language was Latin. By learning Latin, he might go on to a university to become a teacher, diplomat, doctor, scientist, or lawyer. For the Luder family, Martin's good future depended on his learning Latin. So might theirs.

In later years, Martin wrote most of his voluminous writings in Latin. Margaretha and Hans knew they wanted their son to learn Latin. Little did they know how important it would be to his work and to the world.

Magdeburg

Martin was now fourteen years old. He was bright, and his parents kept their hope in him. God was shaping the life of this sensitive son.

For some reason, Hans and Margaretha sent young Martin to the high school in Magdeburg. Shortly after Easter, he left to go north to a city that would open the world of this village boy.

Magdeburg was a city of 15,000 people, larger than any of the cities of Cologne, Ghent, or Paris. Many graves and shrines fanned out from the great cathedral into the surrounding city. The Elbe River brought world commerce, crafts, spices, and beautifully dyed cloth into the city. There were signs of riches

At Mansfeld

Buy a book in Mansfeld, where Luther spent his first school days.

Eat an apple and remember school days.

Talk about school days, especially about early times.

Compare your school days with those of Martin's time.

Look at children and find hope and the future in their eyes and actions.

The Luther family house in Mansfeld

For a housefather who rules his home in the fear of God, training his little children and his servants in the right way, is in a blessed and holy station of life. And a woman who takes care of children by giving them food and drink, wiping and bathing them, need not ask for a holier and godlier position in life. (Luther)

The lowliest day laborer can serve his God as truly as a minister of the Gospel does. (Luther)

To serve God properly means that everyone stay in his calling, however humble it may be, and first heed the Word of God in church, then the word of the government, superiors, or parents, and then live accordingly. This means having served God properly. (Luther)

Martin Luther's first school at Mansfeld

At Magdeburg

Look for the poor, anywhere. Get in touch with your own feelings about them. Have compassion for the poor in a specific way.

Give up something today. Practice self-denial. Be in charge of your willpower.

Pretend to be a small-town child coming into the Dom (the Cathedral Church). Stare and look around.

Hans Luther saves money to buy a foundry.

Hans Holbein the Younger is born. He receives lessons from his father, Hans the Elder, and becomes a famous painter of portraits and religious subjects. He designs many woodcuts, including two famous series: "The Dance of Death" and "The Old Testament."

all around. Primitive people had grown into a clever, wise, joyful, and sophisticated community. There were two parts to the city: the common citizens and the old wealthy. Magdeburg was linked to other major German cities through commerce and through unrest. There was similar unrest among the exploited of Cologne, Hamburg, Rostock, Regensburg, and Augsburg.

Young Martin may not have seen this class distinction, exploitation, and unrest until five years later in Erfurt.

In Magdeburg, Martin enrolled in the high school under the rule and order of the "Brothers of Common Life." This community of laity was without vows, but lived by monastic rules. These Christian brothers loved the Scriptures, prayed freely, and were known to be loving and kind. They lived as a large family.

Many citizens called them the "Null Brueder" or the Zero Brothers. They lived as a commune. They blended the old way of educating with a humanitarian spirit. They were a family of love and learning for young Martin.

Many impressions flooded the mind of the boy from Mansfeld. What may have impressed him most was the Duke of Anhalt, now a beggar in the streets of Magdeburg. He had given up his wealth and status in order to beg daily for alms, as a new way of life. In later years Luther recalled, "When I was fourteen at the school in Magdeburg, I saw him with my own eyes. He lived as a begging monk in Magdeburg. He went barefoot through the wide streets of the city asking for bread, and he carried his sack while bent over like a donkey. He looked like a picture of death, full of hair and bones. All who saw him smacked their lips in prayer and were filled with shame."

The picture of the beggar may have deeply influenced Martin's spirit. Later he told how all stand as beggars before God. All depend on God's grace.

In September, Martin saw his first great religious procession. There was none like it in little Mansfeld. Early in the morning, the faithful began their parade at the Dom. They were joined by the abbot of the Kloister Bergen and the probst of the Church of the Beloved Virgin. The faithful went through the streets carrying candles and holy images, and were led with the banner of St. Mauritz. In the midst of the procession was a silver casket containing such costly relics as earth from Damascus, out of which God made Adam; milk of the Virgin Mary; and the skull cap of St. Francis. At the conclusion of the parade, the faithful knelt in prayer in the giant cathedral

Arrange creative ways to enter the school life of Luther in Mansfeld, Magdeburg, Eisenach, or Erfurt. See how he learned. Tell true school stories.

Create a community to resemble the Brothers of the Common Life, with whom Martin lived when he was thirteen. Find out how persons learn the Scriptures, caring, prayer, courage, and piety.

Imagine a stranger as being royal. See nobility in all persons.

Listen for sounds and look for sights in the city that may have been there during Luther's time.

Look for buildings that were already old when Martin was a child.

Look for something that was built in Luther's lifetime.

Think of your own piety, your own closeness to God, and how this piety became yours.

Magdeburg Cathedral

My idea is to let boys go to such a school for an hour or two a day and spend the rest of the time working at home, learning a trade, or doing whatever their parents desire. In this way study and work may go hand in hand while the children are young and able to do both. They are known to spend at least ten times as much time at shooting peas, playing ball, racing, and wrestling. (Luther)

Just so a girl can surely find time enough to go to school one hour a day and still attend to all her duties at home. She will probably sleep, dance, and play away more time than that. . . . The devil would rather have coarse blockheads and people who are good for nothing, lest men fare too well on earth. (Luther)

If I had children (he later had seven) and could achieve my purpose, they would have to study not only the languages and history but also singing, music, and all the branches of mathematics. . . . How I regret now that I did not read more poets and historians and that no one taught me them! (Luther)

churchyard. Such a procession and such devotion was not a sight he would soon forget.

After one year in school, Martin returned home. Perhaps he did not wish to continue. Or maybe times for his father Hans were poor, and it would be cheaper to send their son to Eisenach, where he might stay with relatives.

Martin was fifteen when he walked from Magdeburg to Mansfeld, a three-day journey. He no doubt walked with others who were traveling in that same direction.

Eisenach

Martin was now fifteen. In Eisenach there was a good high school where Martin would now be a student. Perhaps he could stay with the relatives of his mother, for it would save the family money. On the other hand, Hans could now afford to pay for a better school, for he had become supervisor for several silver mines in Mansfeld.

His parents wanted a good school to challenge Martin's sharp mind. Here in Eisenach he could study philosophy, mathematics, more grammar, and literature. Here he would also learn all subjects in Latin, and if all went well he would go on to a university.

It was a three-day walk south and west from his home in Mansfeld to Eisenach. Beautiful Eisenach, nestled in the hills and forests of Thuringia: It became a second home for Martin. One mile to the south was the Wartburg fortress towering over the hills. This bastion for soldiers helped dukes to protect the southern part of the province of Saxony. Guards, knights, and squires rode gallantly through the hills, and their armor shone brightly against the earthtones of little Eisenach. How brightly the regal banners of nearby Erfurt shone as they fluttered in the wind.

Saxony was one of 300 provinces of the Roman Empire. Most of the Empire covered what is today Germany. One of the soldiers, Duke Frederick the Wise, would soon have Wartburg as one of his Saxon castles.

But in 1498, Luther knew nothing of Frederick, and little of nobles and knights.

In the Cotta family, Martin found free lodging. His singing in a caroling club often served as his pay. He loved music and sang quite well. It was not uncommon for boys to carol through the streets for pennies, sausage, or supper. He received free board from the merchant Schalbe family in exchange for tutoring their son.

1498

Martin goes eighty miles southwest to the Latin School of St. George's, Eisenach. He lives in the elegant, half-timbered Cotta House. Martin spends three happy years with Trebonius, his favorite teacher.

February 16: Philip Melanchton, future teaching friend of Luther, is born.

1499

January: Katherine von Bora is born near Eisenach.

Joy is as necessary to youth as eating and drinking are necessary, for the body is invigorated by a soul that is happy. To be sure, training must be begun, not with the body but with the soul: However, it must proceed in such a way that the body is not neglected. When minds have been correctly instructed, bodies are easily controlled. (Luther)

One should not only serve youth but should also avoid offending them by word or deed. One should give them the best of training that they may learn to pray. (Luther)

At Eisenach

Walk the streets of Eisenach, humming a Luther tune.

Go caroling in the night, as Martin did in school days.

Sing for your supper, even if for the fun of it.

Go slowly through the Cotta House, and feel the simplicity, elegance, and good spirit that shaped the life of adolescent Martin.

Think of teenagers who have similar attributes to Luther's.

Buy a hat and tip it to someone young. Say a silent prayer in their behalf. Honor someone young in some special way.

Luther's coat of arms

Take a photograph of St. George Church. Read or hear the story of how St. George slayed the dragon. Think of Luther struggling with his personal dragon. Compare St. George's struggle, Luther's struggle, and your own.

Take along Luther's Small Catechism in confession or in prayer form and read it in Eisenach.

Smell the air, and feel the atmosphere of being in the Thuringian forests.

1500

Martin has his last semester of high school. In a speech Martin impresses the visiting Professor Trutvetter, from Erfurt University. This perhaps influences his later choice to attend that university.

The building of the Augustinian Hermit Cloister begins in Wittenberg. This will become the Luther House.

The end of the world is expected.

Famous Reformation artist Albrecht Durer carves the "Apocalypse."

The explorer Vasco da Gama reaches India.

The pocket watch is invented by Peter Henlein.

So Martin lived in the lap of a loving family during these three years of adolescence. The pious and cultured household of the Cottas shaped his simple peasant life. Perhaps the childhood stories he was told by his mother would now be revealed to Martin in a new light. The devotion and music in Eisenach would be important in his later life and work. Music would spread the Gospel more quickly than his preaching would. And Wartburg and the Thuringian forest would prove to be a valuable hideaway in twenty years.

Perhaps Martin was most influenced by his teacher Trebonius. With him, Martin learned to feel respect, value, and greatness. Luther recalled how Herr Trebonius would stand and tip his cap as students entered the classroom. Who could know the fame some of them would have one day? Surely this respect inspired excellence in young Luther.

Yet there was plenty to trouble young Martin. His parents mirrored their times. They were typically pious, stern, and demanding. Work and religion were not always joyous. Death was all around them, and the Black Plague was sweeping through Europe like a terrifying whirlwind.

Martin was sensitive and bright. He was increasingly aware of the trouble and strain in his own home, the Church, and the Empire. The times were depicting a stern, righteous, holy God. Popular religious plays like "Everyman" showed death dancing everywhere and before everyone alike—good and bad, queen and nun—to present them before God the Judge.

Martin did not miss seeing and feeling these medieval pictures of God. He would wonder for much of his life if these stories and words were true, and how he could ever find hope and comfort before such a God.

The life in Luther's church stressed Latin, relics of saints, sacrifices of priests, the righteousness and might of God, Christ's suffering, religious processions, saints, spiritual plays from cart stages, fasting, rules and orders, witches, evil spirits, poverty, wealth, and a very real sense of devils. In this, Martin would look for meaning. His cry for help was not uncommon.

Now, in Eisenach, his spirit was becoming a bastion with more might than the thick walls of the Wartburg on the hill.

Erfurt

The University

In 1501, when Martin was eighteen, he enrolled in the University of Erfurt. The school was excellent and also expensive. Hans and Margaretha felt that nothing was too good for their son. Finally their dream was being realized:

Imagine being kidnapped and hurried up the hill into Wartburg Castle. Close your eyes, and pretend to be blindfolded. Identify smells and sounds Luther might have experienced.

Stand still, close your eyes, and be all alone under the ban of the emperor and the Church. There is a bounty on your head, and you are wanted for your life. How do you feel?

Carry a New Testament into the Wartburg Castle, and remember back home that the book was there.

In order outwardly to maintain its temporal estate, the world must have good and skilled men and women, that the former may efficiently rule the country and its people and the latter may efficiently keep house and train children and servants aright. (Luther)

Luther singing for Frau Cotta

Think deeply about people Luther missed while in exile, people whom you miss, and people who miss you.

Focus on one spot you see in the countryside below the castle. Let your mind travel like a spiral into the world. Go from that place into the whole world. Remember where that one spot in Eisenach was.

Woodcut of old Erfurt skyline

Experience teaches us that youths reared with extreme strictness become much worse when loosed from restraint than those who have not been so strictly reared. So utterly impossible it is to improve human nature with commandments and punishments. (Luther)

A young person is like the juice of fruits. You cannot keep it; it must ferment. (Luther)

God has not created us to be arrogant, hard, unreasonable, and boorish but to show honor to one another. (Luther)

At Erfurt

Photograph a tree such as the one Luther may have taken refuge under during the storm. Photograph any storm that may occur.

1501

Luther enrolls at the University of Erfurt, which is a three-day journey from Mansfeld. Erfurt is surrounded by fields of yellow saffron and meadows of blue flax; it is the center of the dye industry. This city of many steeples and monastic communities is also an important religious center. The cathedral and St. Severus stand side by side on a hill called Domberg. The university was founded in 1392 and has 2000 students. Martin is housed in the dormitory, Burse of St. George.

1502

September 29: Luther receives a B.A. degree after two years of study, ranking thirteenth in a class of fifty-seven. He now has the right to wear an academic sword, which nearly causes his death on the way home for a vacation. While recovering from this, he learns to play the lute. He begins an M.A. course at the university.

1503

Julius II becomes Pope.

At age twenty, Luther sees his first Bible in the university library and reads from I Samuel.

1505

The death of Martin's friend is caused by the Black Plague.

Michelangelo is commissioned by Pope Julius II to construct his magnificent papal tomb in St. Peter's of Rome.

Martin would study law. He might even meet a wealthy lady, so he would never have to be poor.

For three years, he studied at Erfurt University. He made many friends and enjoyed long talks with them into the night. Young Martin was learning more and more about the world of religion, politics, and justice. He saw the poor begging in the streets, even crowding the massive stairs before the cathedral.

The terror of the Black Plague visited Erfurt. One of Martin's friends was struck down by the dreaded disease. Martin risked health and life preparing for the burial. In the year 1500, the average life span was twenty-eight years. Martin was now twenty. His life might also be short. Would Martin be ready to meet God? Was studying law a preparation to meet God?

Before going home to Mansfeld for vacation, he had an accident with a sword. Blood poisoning almost caused his death.

All this was on Martin's mind during his vacation. The thought of quitting the study of law could only cause an argument at home. And the dream of his aging parents was now close to coming true.

But Martin's thoughts were on how people prepare to meet God. His thoughts were on salvation. The saving picture of his own baptism in Eisleben must have come to mind, where twenty-one years before, the village priest, his father Hans, and he were in the St. Peter–Paul chapel, and he was one day old. But even that thought could not keep his heart from trembling before death and God. What else could prepare him for the life eternal?

His thoughts were on the end of life. If only Martin could have a daily assurance. . . .

On returning from Mansfeld to Erfurt, a three-day walk, a thunderstorm caught him by surprise. Martin fell to the earth in the peak of the lightning and cried out to the saint of the miners: "Saint Anne, help me, and I will become a monk!" Martin lived. He kept the promise he'd made under the tree in the storm, by the village of Stotternheim, just east of Erfurt.

The Cloister

Martin Luther entered Erfurt to keep his agreement with God. The towering spires of the city, and the unrest among citizens awakening to human prejudice, looked different to Martin this day in July, 1505. Perhaps he could now do something about the gold-plated statues, the hopelessness of beggars, and the fear of the faithful. Maybe as a monk Martin could help himself and others to meet God in sure death.

Save a twig and remember the storm near Stotternheim in which Luther prayed to be saved.

Study the spires of the cathedral against the skyline, and imagine Martin's feelings as at age seventeen he arrived in the city as a student.

See the ornate details of cathedrals, and think of poverty, begging, and the jobless.

Close your eyes and hear monks and Luther chanting, scrubbing floors, begging, and reciting prayers.

Read the Mass, or Holy Communion service, and look for mercy in the words.

Have a sense of awe and mystery in specific places in Erfurt.

Carefully examine a lute or other musical instrument of Luther's day.

The marker indicating where Luther experienced the storm just outside Stotternheim

---

Let the man who would hear God speak read Holy Scripture. (Luther)

What man would be able to speak of repentance and the forgiveness of sins as the Holy Spirit speaks in this psalm? (Luther)

After all, no book, teaching, or word is able to comfort in troubles, fear, misery, death, yea, in the midst of devils and in hell, except this book, which teaches us God's Word and in which God Himself speaks with us as a man speaks with his friend. (Luther)

He who carefully reads and studies the Scriptures will consider nothing so trifling that it does not at least contribute to the improvement of his life and morals, since the Holy Spirit wanted to have it committed to writing. (Luther)

Find a feather or string, or purchase something simple that can be a bookmark for your Bible.

In Erfurt

Remember precisely something important you heard or read. Know it by heart.

July 2: Luther returns to the university after a vacation at home in Mansfeld and is caught in a thunderstorm near the village of Stotternheim, near Erfurt. He calls on Miner's Saint Anne, mother of Mary. He changes plans for his future.

July 17: Luther enters the Augustinian Cloister of Erfurt at the age of twenty-one.

Lucas Cranach is appointed court artist at Wittenberg.

1506

September: Luther takes the monastic vow and becomes a novice.

The reconstruction of St. Peter's Cathedral in Rome begins.

So Martin, now twenty-two, abandoned the hope of being doctor, scientist, or lawyer. The cloister would require celibacy and poverty. Now there would be no rich lady in his life. How heartbroken his parents must have been. And how angry, and how frightened, they must have felt. Now their son would be poorer than the peasant, for the order required the vow of poverty.

His fellow students doubted his announcement. They knew Martin for his sense of humor. They were certain he was joking. Even at the party the night before he entered the thick doors of the cloister, some were not sure.

On July 17, 1505, the heavy doors of the Augustinian cloister shut behind him. He would now be protected, befriended, and baffled behind the heavy walls of this strict monastery.

Martin lived in a cell. In the Erfurt House he lived as a family member with sixty priests and brothers called monks and friars. The House rules were fixed years before by St. Augustine. The rules they all practiced were called their order.

Here Martin spent long hours awake in praying, begging for alms, and doing penance for sins. He did many acts of penance beyond the rules required in the community. Here in the Erfurt House he could finally study the Bible. It was a reason he had chosen this order. Martin wanted to read God's word himself.

A priest, Father John Staupitz, often came from the town of Wittenberg to visit the Erfurt House. He was supervisor of all Augustinian houses, of which the Erfurt House was one. No one listened better or understood with such compassion the struggle of Martin, as did Father John Staupitz. Martin poured out his spiritual questions to him and thought of Staupitz as his own parent.

When Martin was too hard on himself, Staupitz heard him, talked to him, and pointed him to the Scriptures. But Martin was not sure that the Word he heard was loving enough. Together they worked through long lists of sins. Luther could recite these by heart, some of them sins he'd never committed. Luther wanted to be sure that no sin would keep him from eternal life. Staupitz teased, joked, scolded, listened, assured, pled, and instructed serious Martin. Martin Luther respected and heard his Father Confessor, but he did not hear the good Word he wished to hear for his comfort and faith. Martin did not yet see the good picture of God that he could trust on Judgment Day.

A fringe of hair called tonsure circled his head like Christ's crown of thorns. A white yoke hung from his neck like the weight of sin on Christ. His robe was black and was called a

Remember the first Bible you read. Think of how Luther felt when he first read from the Bible in the university library at age twenty.

Touch the earth, a stone, a tree, or a building and be glad for heritage.

Monastery in Erfurt

If we fail to do the works whereby we serve the poor and if we do not interest ourselves in their need, He does not intend to recognize us either. For what we do for our neighbor we do for God and for Christ Himself. (Luther)

Go without a meal and think of fasting. Experience gratitude.

Think of someone unemployed whom you know, and reflect on how it makes you feel. Think what you can do.

Cloister walk in Erfurt monastery

Go to one spot in Erfurt and pray into all four directions. From here, get in touch with the whole world.

If possible, celebrate Holy Communion in Erfurt.

The Holy Spirit has a way of His own to say much in few words. (Luther)

The entire Bible does nothing else than give a person to understand what he was, what he is now, what behooves him, and what his works are. (Luther)

No book but Holy Scripture can comfort us. It alone has the title St. Paul here gives it: the "Book of Comfort." (Luther)

A strong argument for faith in Scripture is this: that only Scripture tells how life goes on and of what a thing consists. (Luther)

For wherever Baptism and the Gospel are, no one is to doubt the presence of saints, even if they were only babes in their cradles. (Luther)

---

cowl. He dressed as he felt: humble, burdened, weighed down.

What if Staupitz had not listened to Martin? But he did listen, and Martin would hear God's own gracious Word. That is why he'd chosen the Erfurt House: to hear God's own Word.

In the monastery, Friar Martin got high marks for devotion, penance, begging, praying, and sincerity. He had given up everything to be sure of salvation. He was doing what the order of Augustine required. And he was doing even more. It was his hope that in this House and in his spiritual hunting would come peace for his life.

The First Mass

Martin had invited his father Hans to the first mass on May 2, 1507. This mass in the Augustinian chapel, over which Martin would preside as president, was the sign that he was now a priest.

His father came with a wagon, drawn by twenty white horses. Did he wish to show his son the world of wealth he'd left behind to enter Augustinian poverty? Or was it a sign of respect for his own son's priesthood? Or did the many horses help bolster his nerve to meet his son? Hans came with the best he had to the festive mass in the Augustinian cloister.

After mass, father and son sat together at the banquet table. Hans again regretted that Martin had left the study of law. How could a poor monk under a vow of poverty care for parents in their old age? Martin argued that he could do more for them with his prayers than if he were a wealthy man. Martin expressed his confidence in his calling, saying that it was of God. Old Hans, in a mood of despair, fired back that the calling might be of the devil. That set up a great doubt in the mind of Martin. Was his calling of God or of the devil?

Martin was deep in search for a loving image of salvation. The popular picture of God was a severe judge on a throne, with heavy feet set on the earth. The picture missing for Martin was the circle of grace, the rainbow, the promise that was in the baptistry twenty-four years ago in the village of Eisleben. He was looking for a new picture of Christ, who was for him and not against him.

Martin had a preoccupation with the end of things, with death and the coming judgment. What he yet had to discover was eternal life as daily renewal.

Martin was not done with God. They were very much on speaking terms, for now Luther had found the Scriptures. There he would surely find the picture that would take away his trembling. Martin was hunting.

1507

May 2: Luther says his first Mass, in fear, at the Augustinian cloister and enters the priesthood.

The Word of God makes the church; it is lord over all places. . . . Where God speaks, where the ladder of Jacob is, where angels ascend and descend, there is the church, there the kingdom of heaven is opened. (Luther)

The only mark of the Christian Church is following and obeying the Word. (Luther)

Humility and reverential fear in the presence of God's Word has ever been the true token of the genuine holy church. (Luther)

The Christian Church is God's maid and servant. It listens to and does nothing but what it knows to be His Word and command. (Luther)

Spires of old Erfurt

Have a party or toast with a few friends. Celebrate, sing songs, enjoy changing work or jobs.

Write to someone who is struggling spiritually.

Write a poem about Erfurt.

The devil is a greater rascal than you think he is. You do as yet not know what sort of fellow he is and what a desperate rogue you are. His definite design is to get you tired of the Word and in this way to draw you away from it. This is his aim. (Luther)

No one understands Scripture unless it is brought home to him, that is, unless he experiences it. (Luther)

Read this saying and think of how you would say it in your own words.

What questions does the saying raise?

Read the saying repeatedly until new thoughts come to mind. Share these with others.

Hear what the saying means to other persons.

Recall the times and seasons that the saying most reminds you of.

1508

Luther lectures one semester at the University of Wittenberg, which is now six years old. Wittenberg, a village of 2000, is one mile long and bounded by the Elbe River and a moat. Luther lives in the new Augustinian cloister at the opposite end of town from Castle Church, now under renovation that was begun in 1490. Classes are held in both the cloister and Castle Church.

1509

Martin Luther is both teacher and student at the university for seven months, and he earns a B.A. in Bible studies.

October: Luther returns to Erfurt to teach for a few months.

Katherine von Bora, age ten, enters the nunnery at Nimschen. Nine years later she will take vows.

Duke Frederick the Wise begins a major relic collection in Castle Church.

Pope Leo X decrees the sale of indulgences for the reconstruction of St. Peter's in Rome.

Henry VIII comes to the throne of England.

1510

Summer: Citizens demonstrate their unrest against the city council of Erfurt.

Wittenberg

Visiting Professor

Father Staupitz, vicar of the Augustinian monasteries in Germany, called Luther to Wittenberg to teach in the winter of 1508. The assignment was only for a semester, but it was the beginning of his search in the Scriptures as teacher. Seven years in Erfurt had helped him to prepare to live in both the Word and in the world creatively.

At the University of Wittenberg, Dr. Staupitz had taught the Bible. He was now getting older and thought it good for young Martin and for the school that Martin should teach there.

The university was less than ten years old. Frederick the Wise wished for his new school to become famous. Soon this young monk, educated in the excellent schools of Erfurt, would attract fame and students to Wittenberg and make it even more excellent than the other German universities. The town of 2000 would boom. The printing presses would multiply and reproduce many volumes of books and tracts that were to come from the pen of this young monk. All the Holy Roman Empire would know the name of Luther as a household word.

Pilgrimage to Rome

In November of 1510, Staupitz sent young Luther and an older priest to Rome to settle an Augustinian dispute. To Rome, the holy city! He went on foot over the Alps to the capital city of the Church. Surely there he could make peace with God. He visited shrines along the way, and worshipped with pilgrims wherever possible. He did penance to be ready for Rome. He ascended the endless steps of Pilate's stairs, as Christ had done. Kneeling, he kissed each step on the way. He made intercession for deceased relatives. Martin saw poor and simple people praying and paying to see and touch relics. He thought: What kind of just God would require such poor to pay so much?

The dispute in the order was settled. But the trouble in his spirit was not yet resolved. What he was looking for he had not found in this visit. Angry and dejected, Martin walked back over the Alps, 800 miles, to report to Staupitz what he had seen—and not seen.

To Wittenberg to Stay

In April of 1511, Luther was called back to the University of Wittenberg to teach Bible and philosophy. Dr. Luther would stay in this city all his life, until he was sixty-two. He was now twenty-eight.

At Wittenberg

Play a musical instrument or do something else musical while in this city.

Sing or read some of Luther's sixty songs with specific events of his life and of your life in mind.

Read Psalm 22 and Romans 1:17 while in or near the Black Tower in the Luther House.

Two towers of City Church at Wittenberg

For a number of years I have now annually read through the Bible twice. If the Bible were a large, mighty tree and all its words were little branches, I have tapped all the branches, eager to know what was there and what it had to offer. (Luther)

It is not the Word of God because the church says so; but that the Word of God might be spoken, therefore the church comes into being. The church does not make the Word, but it is made by the Word. (Luther)

Grammar is to be a servant, not a judge in the Holy Scriptures. (Luther)

All schoolmasters teach that the sense should not serve and follow the words, but the words the sense. (Luther)

The nave of St. Mary's Church in Wittenberg

Create a mini-tour using several rooms as places to visit in Luther's journey. Map out a park, town, or city, and stage the main events of his lifetime. Plan so that people can sense distance, direction, and moods of places.

Plot a Luther pilgrimage, stopping at five or ten devotional Stations. Rest in each Station and reflect on spiritual ideas in Luther's time, and today.

Use chalk to draw Luther information on a sidewalk or parking lot to guide people through history in playful ways. It may resemble hopscotch and other sidewalk games known from childhood.

November: Luther journeys to Rome on business to defend the strict rules of the Augustinian order. He and an older priest travel 850 miles on foot to the Eternal City.

Philip Melanchton at age thirteen enters Heidelberg University to receive his B.A. degree at age fifteen and M.A. at age sixteen.

1511

Early April: Luther returns to Erfurt with his mission accomplished, but he is spiritually depressed.

Late summer: Luther is transferred by Father John Staupitz to Wittenberg to teach the Bible and to study Hebrew and Greek.

He learned Greek and Hebrew so that he could read the Bible in its original language. He loved to teach theology and help people to find ways to think about God. Always he hoped to find the truest picture of God.

Soon students began to write down most everything their dear professor said. Some wrote that his voice was sharp and high, but tender. He spoke clearly. And he wished to understand God's Word more clearly. His image of God was still distorted. The picture of grace was not yet revealed to him.

Dr. Luther was soon to become a famous professor in the new University of Wittenberg. In that city of 2000 citizens, he would spend the remainder of his thirty-four years as preacher, teacher, counselor, parent, and reformer.

He lectured at the university, taught young priests the Scriptures in the Black Tower monastery, and counseled students. Soon it seemed he was writing letters all day long, for many came to trust him. He arbitrated in legal matters, composed music, wrote songs and hymns, and listened to the social concerns of his people. He was assistant to Staupitz and to the prior vicar of the Augustinian monastery in Wittenberg. Dr. Luther was preacher in St. Mary's, the city church.

Luther's Prince

Luther sometimes preached at the Castle Church where Frederick the Wise worshiped. Frederick, duke of Saxony, was one of five princes serving as elector in the cabinet of Charles V, king of the Holy Roman Empire. Over the next fifteen years, in the many political and religious councils, he and Luther never met. Perhaps he could better befriend this exciting monk from a distance. It is reported that Frederick had his seat in the Church tipped back so that he and Luther could never have a face-to-face contact. The prince of Saxony wanted to stay objective in this series of political events.

Elector Frederick had a large collection of relics in the Castle Church. His catalog of relics listed some 10,000 religious items from the whole Christian world. They ranged from hair to milk, from bones to cloth. At certain holidays and fairs, the relics were a main attraction. Their magic and imagery satisfied the minds of uneducated and superstitious people. All of this displeased the young monk. Martin felt these images were not helping people to see the truth about themselves and God.

The emperor was eventually bothered by the young preacher's stand in these matters. These relic exhibitions had become an important fundraising program in the Empire. Martin was in the middle of the argument. Duke Frederick, with all his relics, would protect Dr. Luther, who was now bringing fame to the Wittenberg university.

Talk about the struggle of faith and fear as freely as did Luther. Share in ways that lead to faith and freedom.

Notice the many journeys of life. See the pilgrimage of all nature, of emotions, faith, property, nations, farms, families, and the person. All life is an awesome journey.

I intend to say nothing at this point about the fine, delightful satisfaction a man derives from being educated even if he never holds an office; how at home he can read all sorts of things by himself, how he can talk and associate with learned people, and how he can trade in foreign lands. For in all probability very few are aware of the joy one can derive from being educated. (Luther)

Emperor Charles V as a young man, painted by Albrecht Durer

Turn this saying into prayer.

Try to restate this Luther saying in your own words.

Draw or scribble a picture of this idea. Share your scribblings.

Connect this saying with a poem, song, hymn, or another saying you know.

True it is that human wisdom and the liberal arts are noble gifts of God, good and useful for all kinds of things, wherefore one cannot do without them in this life. But they can never thoroughly tell us what sin and righteousness are in the eyes of God, how we can get rid of sins, become pious and just before God, and pass from death into life. (Luther)

Bronze of Elector Frederick the Wise in the Castle Church of Wittenberg

It would certainly be good if your Grace (Margrave George of Brandenburg) would establish one or two universities at suitable places in your principality where not only the Holy Scriptures but also law and all sorts of arts would be taught. From these schools learned men could be taken to serve as preachers, pastors, secretaries, councilors, and in other capacities for the whole principality. (Luther)

Learning, wisdom, and writers should rule the world; and if God in His wrath were ever to remove all the learned from the world, what would the remaining people be but beasts? (Luther)

1512

October 19: Luther receives a Doctor of Theology degree and becomes a professor of Bible. He finds peace at last by researching Psalms and Romans in his "Stube" in the "Black Cloister."

1513

August 16: Dr. Luther begins lectures on the Psalms.

Leo X becomes Pope.

Albrecht Durer, Dutch artist, creates "Rider, Death and Devil."

1514

Albert von Brandenburg is made Archbishop of Mainz, and later is to be involved with Luther in the indulgence debate.

1515

April 15: Luther is made the Augustinian district vicar for Thuringia and Meissen by Vicar John Staupitz.

Martin Luther accepts a call to be pastor of St. Mary's, the City Church of Wittenberg. He will preach many sermons in this massive, simple, two-towered church.

1516

October 27: Luther begins his lectures on Galatians. He is thirty-three years old.

The regular postal service in Europe is established.

The Black Tower

Though Luther was a priest, had been to Rome, taught the Bible, knew the Church, and was diligent in prayer, he was caught up in spiritual interpretations of the times. He was in many ways a medieval man, and was tuned in to the fears, feelings, and frustrations of the sixteenth century. He was sorting through it all in his room in the monastery of Wittenberg.

Father Staupitz trusted Martin and gave him increasing responsibility as overseer of some of the Augustinian monasteries. Even so, Martin debated questions of faith with his Confessor, Staupitz, and shouted out on occasion that he hated God. So great were his doubts at times. The question his father raised when Martin said his first Mass had not left him: Was his calling into the priesthood of God, or of the devil?

Martin grew in faith just as the biblical images of God unfold. Revelation came gradually to this studious monk. He read the Scriptures over and over to see if he had missed a gracious image. He saw how the Bible interprets itself. It became to him like a giant web and a system of faith. In a turret of the Black Tower, the Augustinian monastery where he lived with thirty other monks and brothers, he searched the Bible daily. He prepared popular lectures on the Psalms, Romans, Galatians, and the book of John. It was in that study that Luther saw the light.

In the Psalms and Romans, the picture grew clear. The common image of the Middle Ages was a God sitting as judge with heavy feet pressed upon the earth. Swords pierced God's cheeks. God was a Lord of wrath. The professor trembled at the thought. He felt the weight and the gloom of the people's hearts.

In Psalm 22, he heard the words of Christ on the cross. He was saying the words that Luther had felt all these years. This Jesus on the cross, God's own Son, was now an outcast and derelict crying the words of Martin. No longer would Martin Luther feel so all alone in despair.

How often Dr. Luther walked from the Black Tower, through the university, south past Melanchton's house, to the City Church, to the Rathhaus for a meeting with Mayor Cranach the artist, and to the Castle Church for special services. But now he stepped differently, for he had a new way of seeing God. He said that with the new sight he had seen, it seemed as though the gates of Paradise had been opened.

Remember that by living in another place, you can get a better eye for what is real and important back home.

Use concrete objects and experiences to get in touch with history and emotions.

Look at differences creatively. Look for causes and social histories that shape life differently. Be constructive as you understand differences, and be open to other ways of thinking and living.

Keep a journal—a notebook or a diary—along the way. Scribble down your impressions, thoughts, feelings. Tape in postcards, photographs, flat souvenirs such as twigs and feathers, tickets, labels, and so on.

Collect and include photographs, sketches, slides, and pictures to help record sights and events. It may be valuable to build a series of photographs around a theme. Good slides, cards, and other souvenirs are available.

The Augustinian Black Cloister, later known as the Luther House in Wittenberg

The living room of the Luther family in the Wittenberg Luther House

The kingdom of Christ consists of those who bear and those who are borne. (Luther)

Truly, the Christian Church on earth has no greater power or work than its joint prayer against everything that may rise in opposition to it. (Luther)

It is impossible for the church to exist without the shedding of blood; for Satan, her enemy, is a liar and a murderer. And the church has always grown by blood; she has been irrigated and planted by blood. That is why it irks me to be obliged to carry my blood to the grave. (Luther)

God help us as He helped our ancestors and will also help our descendents to the praise and honor of His divine name throughout eternity! (Luther)

The Penance Box

Penance was one of the seven sacraments of the Church. Martin Luther thought there were really three: Baptism, Holy Communion, and Penance. Later he would drop Penance from the list.

Penance was a very important exercise in the Church. It was more complicated than merely saying I'm sorry. Penance had these three parts: contrition, confession, and satisfaction.

Contrition meant to be truly sorry for sin. Confession was to tell this sorrow to God. Satisfaction was to do something to show one's sorrow for sin. Luther saw how the Church was distorting and exaggerating the act of satisfaction as a part of Penance. People were required to make satisfaction that was impossible for them. Increasingly, making satisfaction was attached to the act of giving money. It became a way for the Church and the city to pay for welfare work. In Luther's day, it was also a way for the Church to raise money for designated projects.

Penance came to be the key to the Church's treasury. It was now said that saints had a reserve bank account for those in need of Penance. It was a bank of good works, a treasury of merit from which persons could draw merits. Set fees were printed. The Church owned the bank of good deeds.

Speeches hawking this bank account of merits put pressure on the pocketbooks and consciences of the people. Some monks specialized in impassioned speeches urging people to make payments for their satisfaction. People were caught in the emotional plea of this rhetoric.

The year 1515 was declared the Year of Jubilee by Pope Leo X. St. Peter's in Rome needed major rebuilding. Other church debts needed to be paid through the Fuger House Bank of Holland. Monies raised through Penance were called indulgences.

A friar of Saxony, John Tetzel, was brilliant at hawking these indulgences. The price list for indulgences was scaled according to means and to sins. Tetzel and others who hawked indulgences promised people the forgiveness of sin if they paid money and drew on the account of the Church's merit treasure. Varying fees were charged for all possible sins committed in the past or in the future.

Pope Leo enlisted Tetzel to keynote large gatherings and to head up the Jubilee program in the churches near Wittenberg. When this indulgence preacher came into a village, the bells rang, organs played, choirs sang, and processions marched. People were sure they were now securing God's forgiveness.

1517

John Tetzel, Dominican monk from Leipzig, becomes an indulgence salesman, selling indulgences for the Pope and Archbishop Albert of Magdeburg.

October 31: Dr. Luther posts ninety-five theses to the Castle Church door at Wittenberg. He sends a copy to Albert, now both cardinal of Mainz and the archbishop of Magdeburg, who forwards a protest to the Pope.

Look for reconstruction, and talk about what preserving memorials means to you.

Think about what you and your friends can do to encourage and assist in reconstruction.

Consider religious sites and memorials near your home that could be preserved and shared.

Find some meaningful way to bless the town of Wittenberg and any other village or city.

John Tetzel, the Dominican monk who hawked indulgences

Finally we shall speak of those works which a man should do toward his neighbor. For a person does not live for himself alone in this mortal body, as if to work for it alone; he lives for all men on earth; in fact, he lives solely for others and not for himself. (Luther)

No tree bears fruit for itself; a tree gives its fruits to others. In fact, no creature lives for itself and serves itself alone. The sun does not shine for itself; water does not flow for itself. (Luther)

Life has become merely a rough and tough struggle. But this is not the way God has created it. That is not the reason why God let a king, a nobleman, and a rich townsman be born; but He created and gave everything for the purpose of help, benefit, and use that people might serve their fellow men with it. (Luther)

For just as our neighbor suffers want and is in need of our surplus, so we have suffered want before God and were in need of His grace. (Luther)

The wooden pulpit from which Luther preached in St. Mary's Church, the City Church of Wittenberg

Renew a marriage or family commitment while with a spouse, or while alone.

Memorize one of the ninety-five theses and repeat it while at the Castle Church door.

Write your congressman, your elector, and express or support an important idea for peace.

Sing in the Castle Church or in the City Church.

Tetzel quoted from the Scriptures. There was magic in the sermons. Listeners were urged to see and consider their own relatives in the fires of purgatory, a place between death and heaven. Tetzel shamed listeners who would not pay at least a farthing for dead relatives, at least a farthing for the Jubilee indulgence box.

Tetzel is credited with the rhyme: "As soon as the coin in the box will ring, so soon the soul from purgatory will spring."

Penance had become an industry in the Church. People flocked to hear Tetzel. Many from the City Church of Wittenberg walked long distances, especially northeast to Juterborg, to hear the indulgence preacher. Luther was sure they were duped into paying for debts and building programs outside of Germany. The citizens of Germany were being exploited, insisted Luther. Worse, it was heresy. The Gospel is free.

The Jubilee preacher called on people to pay for forgiveness. It may be that the church wanted and needed the money. But in the Scriptures, Martin Luther heard a different message. Forgiveness is free through Christ, said Luther. Forgiveness should not require the poor, or anyone, to give money to take care of the problem of sin.

The Scriptures, not the Church, made this clear to Luther. Grace and faith and the Word are gifts from God alone. Alone became the watchword. Word alone! Grace alone! Faith alone!

The Ninety-Five Theses on the Castle Church Door

Indulgences were the straw that broke the camel's back. Luther's spirit had been pushed too far. Dr. Luther took the debate to his university friends.

By writing the ninety-five theses in Latin, he hoped to test the opinion of the faculty and students. Like all school announcements, his was posted on the north door of the Castle Church. Here students and faculty were sure to see it. That was October 31, 1517.

Within days, the Latin theses were translated into German, and because of the presses, the average citizen was soon reading them. They traveled through Germany within ten days, and throughout the Holy Roman Empire within three weeks.

Pamphlets carried the verbal debate beyond Wittenberg. So many and so angry were the writings that it was called a "pamphlet war." Cartoonists made the debate more vivid and bitter by their own grotesque illustrations. The printing industry increased rapidly in Wittenberg.

Expand a potluck into a Luther feast. Add costumes, music, a tasting table, exhibits, and decoration. End a Reformation course with a history festival.

Use **artistic** ways to restate Luther facts through paintings, poetry, **floral** arrangements, banners, dancing, sewing, ceramics, and music. Facts excite the artist. Show emotion in education. The arts help hold facts together.

The door of Castle Church where theses were posted in Wittenberg

Man performs good works because he has already become a Christian by the new birth through faith, entirely apart from any merits of his own. Therefore it is a settled fact that good works do not make Christians, but Christians produce good works. (Luther)

I believe that there is on earth a holy flock and congregation of pure saints under one Head, Christ, called together by the Holy Spirit in one faith, one mind and understanding, with manifold gifts, yet one in love, without sects and schisms. (Luther)

Therefore also Christ wielded no sword nor instituted any in His kingdom; for He is a king over Christians and rules without law, by His Holy Spirit alone. And though He confirmed the use of the sword, He did not imply it, for it serves no purpose in His kingdom, in which none are but the pious. (Luther)

Photograph sights of nature, people, and places, and see them as symbolic of Luther's journey. See Reformation through the lens of the camera.

Reach boldly into the community and meet a critical issue with the freedom of Luther.

Look for martyrdom today. See whose life is itself the witness. Support the martyr with an act of love.

1518

January: German Dominicans meet in Frankfurt and read 106 theses against Luther, referring their complaint to the Pope.

March: Luther preaches his famous "Sermon concerning Indulgences and Grace."

April, May: Luther is tested by his own Augustinian order in a meeting at Heidelberg.

June: Summons are issued ordering Luther to appear in Rome within sixty days. The summons is received by Luther on August 7. Frederick the Wise arranges instead for a hearing in the Augsburg Congress, or Diet.

October: The Augsburg Congress, or Diet, is held. Cardinal Cajetan, director of the German Dominicans, represents Pope Leo X. Namecalling and hostility prevail. Luther flees Augsburg to return to Wittenberg.

Melanchton is made a professor in Wittenberg and becomes Luther's lifelong friend.

Uhlrich Zwingli begins reformation in Switzerland. He will later encounter Luther in debate in the Castle of Philip of Hesse.

There was to be no stopping the debate. What had begun as an announcement in Latin on a university bulletin board was now a common debate in every German home. The opinions and writings of Martin Luther reached to Rome, to France, and to England.

What Luther had done was well timed. Many things were ready and waiting to happen. German towns were fed up with being exploited. They did not know how to make their next move. Even educated persons felt intimidated and in need of a spokesman. Spiritual people wanted to know the true Gospel. The poor and oppressed were at their wit's end. They looked for a compassionate champion. Peasants were awakening and wanted a better life. Dukes, princes, and their castles were losing prestige and power. Monasteries were losing their influence. A revolution was emerging in almost every German city.

The printing press was only fifty years old and eagerly awaiting news. Cartoonists and satirists were looking for trends and issues. Wittenberg became a printer's haven. The Reformation had many avenues through which to move.

Martin Luther was thirty-four and already a monk of great fame. Wittenberg was on the lips of the whole Empire.

Diets and Councils

Emperor Maximilian and Pope Leo X felt the pressure of the debate on the ninety-five theses. Many cried out that Luther was a heretic. If so, he could be tried and burned.

A series of councils or diets were the next step to come. These were held in 1518 and 1519. Dr. Luther would have to defend his ninety-five theses. The first council, or diet, was at Heidelberg. It was called by Luther's own Augustinian order. They wished to hear out their own member, Martin. Some agreed with Luther. Older priests rejected his position. Many young priests agreed with Luther and took heart. The case, however, was not settled.

In the same year, Luther was called to Rome for trial by Pope Leo X. However, elector Frederick the Wise of Saxony argued that this problem could be solved in Germany. So the council met in Augsburg to debate the matter. Cardinal Cajetan was appointed to represent the Pope. Little was settled. Martin could feel the flame of a martyr's fire.

In the spring of 1519, he was called to a third diet, in Leipzig, sixty miles south of Wittenberg. Many university students walked with him to the diet to support him. This was the scene of Dr. Luther's hopeless debate with Professor Eck. Preceding the debate, there was a grand procession, followed

Remember someone who is special to you and write the words and emotions that come to mind.

Ask for something that you need and become even more aware of how it feels to receive.

Give something to another, expecting no return or thanks. Give with no strings attached.

Sing a tune softly in a cathedral and remember that you sang there.

St. Thomas Church in Leipzig

God's people and the church are those who rely on nothing else than God's grace and mercy. (Luther)

It is impossible to bring the Christian Church together at one place; rather it is scattered throughout the world. It believes as I believe, and I believe as it believes. No difference or inequality of faith exists between us. (Luther)

What kind of spirit is revealed in this saying?

What is the key word for you in this saying?

Allow the saying to begin a conversation.

Turn this particular Luther saying into a poem.

Relate the saying of Luther to someting that recently happened to you.

Every Christian, particularly everyone who is administering a public office in Christendom, should at any time, if the need arises, be personally prepared to stand up, to confess his Lord Christ, and to defend his faith. (Luther)

Although our faith is to rest solely on God's Word, it is nonetheless comforting to know that it is witnessed to in the church. (Luther)

Professor Eck, who debated Luther

1519

June: Charles V of Spain, grandson of Maximilian, is crowned the new emperor of the Holy Roman Empire.

June 27: The Leipzig Debate is held, in which Dr. Luther and Dr. Andreas Carlstadt, faculty dean of Wittenberg University, were tested by Professor John Eck of the University of Ingolsadt, representing the Pope. Because of the large attendance, the meeting was moved from St. Thomas Church to the auditorium of Leipzig Castle.

John Froben of Basel reports the ninety-five theses sold out, with over 600 copies sold to France and Spain.

1520

May: Luther preaches his "Sermon on Good Works."

Emperor Maximilian I dies and Karl V, Charles V, is chosen successor.

June 15: Pope Leo X signs a papal bull, or document, charging Luther to be a traitor. He is given sixty days to take back all he has said, or to be summoned for trial. Erfurt students throw posted copies into the river. Torgau students tear down posted copies and smear documents with mud.

August: Luther publishes the "Address to the German Nobility."

October: Luther writes the popular "Babylonian Captivity."

November: Luther publishes "On the Freedom of Christian Man."

by Holy Communion. Luther was offended by these preliminary celebrations. The meeting was filled with intimidation and namecalling. The shouts of "Heretic!" grew louder. He was hurried back to Wittenberg, still under the protection of Duke Frederick. The duke was not eager to lose this brilliant professor from Wittenberg's growing university.

Manifestos

The "Pamphlet War" grew stronger. The printing presses were busy for many hours of the day and night. Written platforms were published and public stands were taken.

It was now time for manifestos (legal documents or public stands). Dr. Luther's manifestos became for many a declaration of independence.

One manifesto was meant to liberate the duke, duchess, servant, and peasant alike. It was a labor document entitled "To the Christian Nobility of the German Nation." Luther referred to all working people as nobility. Spinners, tailors, seamstresses, bishops, and peasants were all noble before God. All had the right to be educated. Priests should have the privilege to marry. To learn the Scriptures was the right of the entire community. This manifesto demanded full rights and respect for all levels of persons.

Another manifesto warned that the Church was in captivity. This manifesto was titled "On the Babylonian Captivity of the Church." Simple church members were not to be like slaves of religious leaders. Luther said that the sacraments of God have set us free. Baptism and the bread are signs of forgiveness. The people should be released from the bondage of sacramental rules. Christ's resurrection sets all free. All are equal. Christ makes all to be neighbors. Religious leaders have no right to enslave the spiritual lives of the faithful. The document rang like a freedom bell. The refrains "Word alone, grace alone, faith alone" echoed through the whole Church.

Other documents were also published during this time. 1520 was a year of many freedom manifestos. A papal law was sent out against Luther. It began as a psalm to God: "Exsurge Domine." ("Arise, O Lord.") It said that a wild boar would destroy the vineyard. The free spirit of Martin appeared to some as a wild spirit to be captured.

This summons or warning, "Exsurge Domine," meant that Luther was under arrest. He showed the document to university friends who walked together to the city gate of Wittenberg to build a bonfire. Into the fire they threw all documents which they opposed. Then Martin threw in the summons papers. The "Exsurge Domine" went up in flames. Perhaps the Reformation was born in that bonfire of 1521.

Think of someone you influence greatly and how important that is.

Find a feather as a sign of Luther's pen and the great amount of writing done by his hand. See the pen or quill as a sign of peace in times of struggle.

A tract from the Pamphlet War

Your work is a very sacred matter. God delights in it, and through it He wants to bestow His blessing on you. This praise of work should be inscribed on all tools, on the forehead and the face that sweat from toiling. . . . Thus a pious farmer sees this verse written on his wagon and plow, a cobbler sees it on his leather and awl, a laborer sees it on wood and iron: "Happy shalt thou be, and it will be well with thee." (Luther)

It would certainly be a good exercise of faith to learn to pray to God only for the bread of today, so that one might trust in a greater God. (Luther)

God uses our labor as a sort of mask, under the cover of which He blesses us and grants us what is His, so that there is room for faith and we do not imagine that by our own efforts and labors we have achieved what is ours. (Luther)

It is true, of course, that God could support you without work, could let fried and boiled foods, corn, and wine grow on the table for you. But He will not do this. He wants you to work and to use your reason in this matter. (Luther)

Labor you should, but supporting and providing for you belongs to God alone. Therefore you must keep these two very far apart—as far apart as heaven and earth, as God and man. (Luther)

"Thou Shalt Not Steal," painted by Lucas Cranach, artist and mayor of Wittenberg

Allow the saying to penetrate your imagination, and permit images and pictures to come to mind. Compare your images with those of other persons.

If this saying of Luther is important where you live, who are some persons you think are making it happen?

When do you feel the way Luther must have felt as he made this statement?

How does this saying affect behavior?

1521

January 3: A church ban is issued against Luther.

Charles V, age twenty, arrives in Germany.

March: Luther is summoned to the Diet, or Congress, at Worms, and is given a letter of safe conduct.

April 2: Luther and a small group begin the 300-mile journey from Wittenberg to Worms. Herr Sturm leads the procession, on horseback, with the imperial banner. Martin Luther rides in a two-wheeled, horsedrawn cart, singing and playing the lute. In Leipzig, admirers touch the cart and cheer. At Weimar, Justus Jonas joins the party. In Erfurt, the faculty give Luther a hero's welcome, a banquet, and lodging in the cloister. Two thousand admirers line the streets of Worms, cheering Luther.

April 17: At four P.M., Luther is called to St. John's Court, and then taken to a courtroom in the palace to appear before the Parliament, or Reichstag, of church and state leaders. Emperor Charles V is present. Luther delivers his famous defense statement: "Here I Stand."

April 19: Luther leaves Worms for home, under the protection of the emperor.

At Worms

In 1521, Martin Luther was called to defend himself before the new emperor of the Holy Roman Empire, Charles V. Luther would also attend the diet, or parliament, at Worms. He promised Luther a safe trip to and from the council. There was a bounty on Martin's head, and it was not safe for him to travel without disguise or protection. For many, he was on the Empire's most-wanted list.

A friend named Von Hutten, a scholar and knight, begged to march Luther into Worms with a troop of soldiers. He hoped it might begin a war of independence. Luther refused Von Hutten's offer. He said that the Gospel did not need a war to carry out the work of Christ.

In Worms on April 16, 1521, crowds awaited Martin Luther. His name was whispered like that of a hero. Some spoke of him as a heretic.

He was soon to be called before Emperor Charles V. The new emperor was only twenty-five; Martin Luther was thirty-eight. His books and pamphlets were piled before him. He was asked to reject the writings that were his own. He saw they were his, but refused to reject them. He needed time for reflection and prayer. They granted him another day's time.

Torches lit up the palace hall. The room was crowded. Martin began a speech defending his writings. He was urged to get to the point. His answer is reported to be these strong words: "Here I stand. I cannot do otherwise. God help me. Amen."

Some have recorded his words as follows: "I cannot and I will not recant anything, for to go against conscience is neither right nor safe. God help me. Amen."

Many burst into cheers. There was confusion, protest, and shouting. A meeting was rescheduled. Luther was asked to reconsider, but no agreement was reached. A verdict and edict would follow in ten days.

Luther had already been excommunicated by the Pope; he was a heretic. But now he was banned by the emperor; he was an outlaw. Martin was a criminal and a heretic at the mercy of the public.

He was given eight days of protection to get home to Wittenberg. After that, he was to be at the mercy of the public. Anyone who befriended him could be harassed, imprisoned, and condemned. His works were to be destroyed.

Faith receives the good works of Christ; love does good works for the neighbor. (Luther)

If for this or that position you have a grace or gift your fellow Christian does not have, use it in such a way that he is served by it. Do not be puffed up because of it, and do not despise him who does not have gifts of this kind. In this way you wash his feet as Christ has commanded. (Luther)

God has created us to be stewards of our fellow man, but I dare say this is a debt none of us ever fully discharge. However, we Christians have the advantage that we recognize this and feel sorry about it. (Luther)

A Christian must act like a good apple tree, which offers and displays its fruits to everyone and even distributes them among the swine and bad beasts that tear at its roots. (Luther)

Christ has not taught me to be a Christian to the injury of others. (Luther)

The foot moves and supports the body to keep the eye from sustaining an injury. One member is always careful about, and serves, the other rather than itself. (Luther)

Cathedral at Worms

Gather and create an original Luther float. Enjoy information. Learn while playing. Combine skills. See the float as a conversation piece.

Carve pumpkins using Reformation signs and words. Create Luther events in the carvings, and have a journey by candlelight.

Host a sixteenth-century Luther party in which the Luther family and friends attend. Or have a masquerade and ball attended by personages living in Luther's time. It may be simple or elaborate. The persons may include Luther's friends, peasants, nobility, Leonardo da Vinci, Columbus, and others, either famous or not.

Share slides and movies of journeys to Luther's Germany. Hear and see true journey stories.

Luther at the Diet of Worms

May 4: After six days into the journey home, Luther is kidnapped near Eisenach. The arrangement is a protection staged by George Spalatin, secretary of the elector Frederick the Wise. Luther is taken from the cart in the night and carried by horseback through the dark forest into Wartburg.

May 26: The Edict of Worms is signed; Luther is a heretic to the church.

All Saints' Day: Luther's friend Justin Jonas visits the Castle Church and calls all indulgences "rubbish." Unrest is astir in Wittenberg. Other friends of Luther, like Philip Melanchton and Andreas Carlstadt, report wide-reaching changes.

December: Luther begins to translate the Bible, and completes the German New Testament in 100 days.

Mid-December: Luther as Junker Georg (Knight George) makes a secret trip to Wittenberg. He is disturbed and advises against radical changes being made.

Christmas Day: Dr. Carlstadt offers 2000 people both bread and wine in Communion.

Luther had been in Worms for ten days. On April 26, he had left for Wittenberg. They had now traveled six days. Luther was asleep in a cart rolling through the Thuringian hillside about 200 miles northeast of Worms. It was night, near Eisenach, near the place of his mother's birth. Duke Frederick's plan was to protect Dr. Luther until the hostility had settled.

Wartburg

During his trip home from Worms, Luther was kidnapped in the woods outside Eisenach. In the night, friends hurried him on horseback through thick woods, zigzagging their way to finally reach the fortress on the hill. For ten months, he was in hiding in Wartburg.

Immediately rumors spread that Luther had disappeared, perhaps been killed. Maybe he had been forewarned. It was Duke Frederick's plan that Luther be protected from the current rage against him in the empire.

Back home in Wittenberg, many grieved the loss. Albrecht Durer, the Dutch artist, was sure his friend was dead. He wondered who would now tell the Gospel to the people.

Luther was camouflaged as Junker Georg, with a beard and in knight's clothing. So while hiding from the emperor, he was in fact in the emperor's army. In the garrison assigned to Wartburg, Luther was seldom unattended.

Junker Georg lived in the stableman's quarters. From this small room, he could see the smoke of the mining pits rise over the village of Eisenach. From there he saw the place where he once lived with the Cottas and had studied with Trebonius twenty years before.

Martin was often lonely in Wartburg. Temptation, sickness, and despair plagued him. He was often distressed and found comfort in writing about his feelings to friends. He wrote Melanchton, a young colleague in Wittenberg, about his fear of laziness and idleness. He begged that the Holy Spirit might inspire him in this castle prison. His prayer was answered.

Luther overflowed with energy. In the tiny stableman's room, the "Kutcher's Stube," he would write a book that the German people could read: the New Testament in the German language. He knew his Greek and Hebrew. And he knew the individual dialects of students from all over the German-speaking world. From these he created a German translation that all could read and understand. With the common people on his mind, Luther was spurred on. In three months, he translated the entire New Testament into a magnificent German. Now the German people could read God's word for themselves.

Feed the castle's birds and realize how they have been enjoyed through the centuries. Allow the journeys of birds to stimulate your imagination of time and space.

Think of how J. S. Bach felt 200 years later living in Eisenach and reading the works of Luther as inspiration for his music. Discover how poetic Luther's writings are.

Read, whisper, whistle, or sing "A Mighty Fortress" while in or near the Wartburg Castle. Think of the fortress images in the castle and its location, which Luther used in the hymn.

Think of the varied stages of history in the long life of Wartburg Castle.

Ask each other about what you saw and felt today.

Drawbridge at Wartburg Castle

. . . The book of Psalms is a sweet, comforting, lovely song, because it sings and preaches the Messiah, although one merely reads or recites the words without notes. (Luther)

Thus David, too, often dispelled, or at least checked or weakened, the evil spirit for Saul with his minstrelsy. For the evil spirit is not at ease when one sings or preaches God's Word in true faith. He is a spirit of sadness and cannot stay where a heart is spiritually joyful, that is, joyful in God and His Word. (Luther)

Light a candle in memory of Martin and other persons of faith.

Read prayers of Luther, prayers about life, birth, and death. Read them in a special place and with special persons, so you will remember the readings and the praying.

I have constantly striven to produce a pure and clear German translating; and it often happened that for two or three or four weeks we sought and asked for a single word and sometimes did not find it even then. (Luther)

I have translated the New Testament to the best of my ability and according to my conscience. (Luther)

Holy Scripture is full of divine gifts and virtues. (Luther)

The Luther Study (Stube) in Wartburg Castle

From the Wartburg fortress, Luther would continue the Reformation with ink. Freely he wrote letters to leaders of church and state. He corresponded with artists, politicians, theologians, and friends. He began to write sermons and prayers for young preachers. His pen and ink was a mighty weapon against Satan. He threw his inkwell against the Tempter. It was his writing that he threw against the wall where Satan was.

Disguised as the knight Junker Georg, Luther sometimes rode on horseback to Wittenberg. On one occasion, his friend Lucas Cranach painted the portrait "Junker Georg." Luther stayed in touch with church and state events of Wittenberg and the Empire.

Once Swiss students traveling to Wittenberg to hear Dr. Luther lecture stopped at the Black Bear Cafe near Wartburg, in Jena. Junker Georg was eating in the cafe that night. He invited them to his table and told them they'd not find Dr. Luther there. He urged them to go on to Wittenberg to hear the lectures of Dr. Melanchton, and to study Greek and Hebrew. He paid for their meal and left. Later, Herr Kessler, the owner, confided that they'd been with Dr. Luther.

On May 4, 1521, Luther had arrived at Wartburg; it was March 1, 1522, before he returned home to Wittenberg. These ten months in the isolated Thuringian fortress were filled with emotion. Bats and demons wheeled and sped through dark rooms haunted with witches and spirits. They made loud noises like that of bowling balls and beer barrels thumping down wooden stairs. Locked into his close quarters, deep and high inside the fortress, Martin was sometimes very alone. He was often overcome by forces and apparitions of evil. Despair set in. Why must he, a man of faith, hide in his own dear Germany?

Luther and his friends prayed for the Holy Spirit to quiet his spirit. He received a bountiful measure of grace in these ten months. He found purpose and power while in the castle. Martin Luther would no longer be afraid of any enemy, against himself or against the people. Martin had a reformed spirit. The Wartburg fortress was now in Luther's heart.

Reform and Revolution

While Luther was at Wartburg, the Reformation took charge in Wittenberg. For many it sounded the alarm: change, break, destroy, revolt.

For Luther, to reform did not mean to break or destroy. He was dismayed that his friend Andrew Karlstadt, pastor at the

1522

January: The Wittenberg town council passes a law for all images to be removed from churches, and both bread and wine will be given to all people at Communion.

Luther is again disguised as Junker Georg and makes many escorted excursions into the countryside.

March: Luther is concerned about the unrest and social problems in Wittenberg. He returns to Wittenberg to preach and to counsel, in hopes to end the Wittenberg unrest.

September: The first edition of Luther's New Testament in the language of the German people is published.

February 26: Justus Jonas, minister of the Castle Church, marries.

Dr. Carlstadt is banished from Saxony by the Elector Frederick the Wise for urging revolution.

You should keep worrying and working apart. . . . Worrying is forbidden; working is prescribed. (Luther)

Before one has scaled the height, everybody wants to sit on top. But once a person is there, holds the office, and should do what is right, he finds what it really means to hold office and sit on top. For he will be so burdened with work that he thinks: I wonder, did the devil bring me into this office? (Luther)

Worry is forbidden, but not work. In fact, we are commanded and enjoined so to work that the perspiration flows over our nose. God does not want man to be idle. (Luther)

Do not look at your unworthiness; look at the command of God. Do not argue whether you are worthy or not worthy, but hold to the promise that God will do the will of those who fear him. (Luther)

People who are thoroughly versed in spiritual matters have said that praying is harder than any work. (Luther)

Woodcut of Junker Georg by Lucas Cranach

What significance does this saying have for today?

Whom do you often quote? Who is the author of some of your favorite sayings?

Who quotes your sayings? Who listens most carefully to you?

Why is it important to listen to what another individual says?

Luther's room (Stube) at Wartburg Castle

For what could be more pleasing to God and more beneficial to men than so to live in your calling (Beruf) that God is thereby honored and that by your example you bring others to love God's Word and to praise His name? Likewise, what virtues are more useful in the whole life of a man than modesty, meekness, patience, and living in harmony with people? (Luther)

Christian liberty frees souls, and Christ is the Founder of that spiritual liberty which one does not see. (Luther)

Think of old Hans Luther as a spokesman in his church. Do the same for your church. Talk about those who speak up in the church.

1523

Luther writes "On Civil Government" and "On the Order of Worship."

Hans Sachs, poet of Nuremberg, describes Luther as "The Wittenberg Nightingale."

April: A nun, Katherine von Bora, and eleven other nuns, leave the Nimschen convent of Grumma and arrive in Wittenberg, perhaps in herring barrels. Luther cares for their welfare, safety, and future.

July: Two Augustinian monks leave their Brussels monastery and are caught, tried, and burned. They are the first martyrs of the Reformation.

1524

January, February: Luther writes "To the Councilmen . . . Christian Schools."

Erasmus of Rotterdam, influential humanist and reformer, publishes his famous "On the Freedom of the Will."

June: The German Peasant War begins.

The English reformer William Tyndale visits Luther in Wittenberg. In 1526 his English New Testament is printed in Worms and is smuggled into England. Soon after, Tyndale is burned at the stake.

Dr. Luther preaches in the City Church of St. Michael's in Jena. His original tomb plate can be seen there today.

Castle Church, was also stirring up the congregation. Luther felt the reform was too drastic and violent.

Monks were leaving monasteries. The Augustinian community in the Black Tower was dwindling. Priests were also giving the cup to the people in Communion. That was new. Clergy refused to wear their ornate robes. That was alright with Luther. Some broke their fast days. Mobs broke into churches, tumbling statues and smashing ornate windows. That was new. Clowns interrupted the mass with silly sayings, disturbing singing and worship. So much was new and destructive.

It was high time for Junker Georg to come back to Wittenberg as Dr. Luther. He returned to stop this destruction and nonsense. For eight days, he preached and begged the congregation to stop the disgrace. Wittenberg was quieted by the Gospel. Reform was not meant to be violent.

But the debate continued, and it was not all pleasant. Cartoons exaggerated issues. Crude illustrations spoke vividly and bluntly to uneducated people. Professionals drew lines with animosity. The exchange of pamphlets (Flugschriften) between Luther and opponents was a heated battle. It was a global debate, a paper warfare: the "Pamphlet War." The same cartoonists sketched for both sides of an issue. They outdid themselves with crudeness. Luther and the Pope were both sketched as deformed monsters and as harlots. Luther objected to these cartoons. There was no control over the free press releases. Printers grabbed the writings while they were being spoken, or while wet with ink. Within days, they were read and viewed through the whole Empire. The new mail system was certainly working.

Reform

What was the distinguishing feature of reform? Luther claimed that the Word of God did everything. The Word was the force; Martin was the instrument. Sometimes the word was against his own will. Luther stayed close to the Scriptures. The Word of resurrection and forgiveness was the force.

Who would be the priest of the Evangelical congregations? Who would lead the Evangelicals, as they came to be called? Who would lead the Luther followers? Many had read the manifesto in which Luther said all are equal, the bishop and the maid. So the people would choose the minister. The Evangelical provinces, cities, and parishes would choose their pastors. The minister would be one called out of their midst; one from the congregation would be minister. Some were former priests, and some were merchants. Before God, all are noble.

Construct a Wartburg Castle to feel its grandeur, age, strength, isolation, and protection. Make it of wood, sand, tinker toys, blocks, or papier-mâché. Libraries will have more details on medieval castles.

Play and sing the great Luther hymns in unusual ways. While some hum, others can say words aloud. Play Luther hymn tunes on the flute, saxophone, or electric guitar. For Luther, music was close to the Scriptures and to the culture of the people. Create a Luther band of all ages.

The castle and Castle Church in Wittenberg

God has instituted three estates. These He has commanded not to let sin go unpunished. The first estate is that of the parents. They should exercise a strict control over their house and rule the children and the household. The second estate is that of the government. A magistrate bears the sword in order to compel the disobedient and the wayward by force to conform to the law or suffer its penalty. The third estate is that of the church. It governs by the Word. So God has protected the human race by this threefold authority against the devil, our flesh, and the world, to the end that offenses may not develop but be prevented. (Luther)

Although God does regenerate believers in Christ to eternal life, yet He retains the station of father, mother, children, lords, servants, and maids in the world and will not allow the estate of matrimony or other estates to disappear. (Luther)

If obedience is not rendered in the homes, we shall never have a whole city, country, principality, or kingdom well governed. For this order in the homes is the first rule; it is the source of all other rule and government. (Luther)

St. Mary's at Wittenberg where Luther preached

Face the direction of your home and say the Lord's Prayer. Perhaps you can say, hear, or read it in German.

Imagine Luther and the congregation of St. Mary's together at Christmastime. Have a quick Christmas in the City Church.

Think through what you believe and be ready to say it or write it into single statements. Think of what some of your ninety-five theses are.

1525

April: Luther writes the "Admonition for Peace."

May: Luther publishes an unreasonable statement, "Against the Plundering and Murdering Hordes," urging the princes to put down the rebellion. Five thousand peasants are killed and six hundred are taken prisoner in the Battle of Frankenhausen. It is the end of the Peasant War. In Thuringia 100,000 peasants and soldiers die. Seventy cloisters and two hundred and seventy castles are destroyed. The peasants gain no rights and will have nothing to say politically or socially for 300 years.

Luther writes "The Enslaved Will."

May: Frederick the Wise dies, and Luther preaches a sermon in the Castle Church. The bronze grave marker is sculpted by Peter Vischer the Younger. The new elector, Duke John the Steadfast, is a close friend of Luther's.

No more ornate robes for priests; now simple black academic robes for ministers of the Word. Simplicity was in. Being pastoral counted. All signs pointed toward understanding the Scriptures.

No more Latin for the Mass; now worship was in the mother tongue, German, a Word that all could understand.

No more priestly office. No more sacramental mysteries; now there would be more shepherding, preaching, and educating.

No more the priest drinking the cup of wine alone. Now all the communicants would take bread and drink the cup. Both kinds were for all.

All are noble, Pastor Luther said. All are to drink, understand, hear, read, and sing. All are to minister. This will keep reform alive. The people are somebody royal; all are priests.

No more choirs of monks chanting plainsong and Gregorian intonations in Latin. Now there were simple melodies and tunes. All the people sang the Gospel in their German tongue.

Martin Luther did more for reform with singing than was done by all the debates. The single act of worship, the people singing, carried the Word into the hearts of the people. Through singing, the new Word of grace spread quickly. The gap between the people and the Word was closing. The Word was in the music. For Luther, next to good theology, good singing was needed.

New music was emerging in Italy, France, Belgium, Holland, and now Germany. People began hearing fifths and thirds, melodies and tunes, harmony and chords. Before, music was in octaves, plainsong, and haunting chants. Now came melody.

Martin loved music. He played the lyre, a guitar-like instrument. He knew popular songs and borrowed their tunes to launch new hymns. Martin knew many folksongs. The new hymns became new spiritual folksongs for many of the people. These melodies spoke the language and concerns of pious people. The folk spirit would find its way into the Church's music. Folk music and melodies soon carried the Word of God. Then came melodious German chorales. The Gospel Luther had found in Scriptures had now found music. There as a spiritual dynamic in the Holy Roman Empire. It was the wind of music blowing out of Saxony.

Winds blow peace, and winds blow storms. Problems abounded among new congregations and Evangelical cities. Would the leaders know the Word? Would ministers study the Scriptures? Would parents and pastors know how to educate? Would there be understanding and Gospel in the preaching? How educated were the new leaders?

I place music next to theology and give it the highest praise. And we see how David and all saints put their pious thoughts into verse, rhyme, and songs, because music reigns in times of peace. (Luther)

Music is a very fine art. The notes can make the words come alive. It puts to flight every spirit of sadness, as is written of Saul. . . . Princes and kings must support music and the other arts too; for although private people love them, they cannot support them. (Luther)

I greatly desire that youth, which after all, should and must be trained in music and other proper arts, might have something whereby it might be weaned from the love ballads and the sex songs and, instead of these, learn something beneficial and take up the good with relish, as befits youth. (Luther)

As someone reads parts of the Luther journey, scribble or sketch simple impressions. With these visual notes, tell the Luther story with imagination and feeling.

Learn ten facts of Luther's early life and compare life then with similar early life events today.

Music is God's greatest gift. It has often so stimulated and stirred me that I felt the desire to preach. (Luther)

When sadness comes to you and threatens to gain the upper hand, then say: Come, I must play our Lord Christ a song on the organ; for Scripture teaches me that He loves to hear joyful song and stringed instruments. . . . If the devil returns and suggests cares or sad thoughts, then defend yourself with a will and say: Get out, devil, I must now sing and play to my Lord Christ. (Luther)

Junker Georg in a detail from the Cranach altar painting in Wittenberg

Luther the musician

Learn to recite some or all of the German alphabet.

Memorize a simple prayer in German.

Write the name of Martin Luther by using German script.

Share something with someone, and view the other person as a sister or brother in Christ.

June 13: Martin Luther and Katherine von Bora are betrothed and marry two weeks later. Katie has chosen Martin over Dr. Glatz or Dr. Amsdorf of Magdeburg, who attends the wedding celebration.

Dr. Luther with friends led a visitation through towns and the countryside to test leaders. Luther was appalled at the ignorance he found. He was sure of this: They needed a Catechism. Their houses needed wall charts with questions and answers on faith. There were other Catechisms in Germany. But they were cumbersome, wordy, and often insulting to the readers. They argued more than they taught. They scolded instead of simply telling. For years, Luther had preached on the commandments, prayer, and faith. These sermons became the base for a lengthy Catechism, which he wrote in 1529: the Large Catechism. Its chief parts were the commandments, the Creed, the Lord's Prayer, the sacraments, and the office of the keys. In the same year, he wrote the Small Catechism. Little did Luther know that this tiny book would never go out of print. Katie once told Martin: "The Catechism tells me all I need to know about myself and God."

Marriage and Family

Luther saw that the world around him was changing very quickly. He was sometimes frightened by the speed of the reform. He begged for patience. The greatest reform of all for Martin was marriage.

In 1523, a group of nuns arrived in Wittenberg. One report was that they'd been smuggled from the convent inside a herring barrel. One of the nuns was Katherine von Bora, then twenty-four years old.

Dr. Luther worried for the welfare of the nuns. His own words had been smuggled into their convent and had given them the nerve and freedom to leave. Would they be safe? Would they be exploited? Who would care for them?

Martin looked among his own friends for possible marriage partners for the nuns. Martin was a matchmaker, for the nuns needed marriage. A good husband could be their security. Luther found husbands for all except Katherine. While he thought she would marry his good friend Glatz, she preferred Martin as a mate.

First Martin went home to Mansfeld for his parents' consent, as was the custom at the time. In June of 1525, Martin and Katie began the marriage that would bring them happiness for twenty years. She was twenty-six and he was forty-two.

As was often the case, the marriage was in some ways a matter-of-fact affair. It was done partly for convenience. Love could grow and come later—and it did. For Martin, it was also a public act to defy those in the Church who forbade marriage. It showed that Luther favored marriage for the clergy. The love

Greet someone who lives in Wittenberg and let them know you like their city. Discover how they feel about living in Luther's town.

Write a note home and tell someone how you felt today about something important.

Katie and Martin's marriage

Precisely speaking, matrimony is based on the mutual consent of man and woman. (Luther)

To be married and to understand married life are two very different matters. He who is married but does not understand married life can never live in it without displeasure, trouble, and misery. . . . He who understands it finds in it delight, love, and joy without ceasing, as Solomon says: "Whoso findeth a wife findeth a good thing." (Luther)

He wants it honored, maintained, and conducted by us, too, as a divine, blessed estate, because He instituted it first, before all others; and with it in view, He did not create man and woman alike, as is evident, not for lewdness, but that they should live together, be fruitful, beget children, and nourish and rear them to the glory of God. (Luther)

Katherine Portal of the Luther House in Wittenberg

Meet as family or extended family and have table talks. Talk about sixteenth-century topics that are still current, related to family, faith, poverty, fear, peace, death, discrimination, and the Bible. Read from Luther's table talks. Write down each other's sayings and be remembered.

Appreciate details within the Luther emblem. Create personal and group emblems that communicate values.

Focus a family or group project on issues of justice and peace, which were important in the sixteenth century, and are still important today. Make a decision together.

If Christ is to be found in life with the neighbor, then consider the neighbor. Plan a neighborhood meeting. Find Christ in the neighbor.

between them grew. How surprised this monk was to wake in the morning and see pigtails on the pillow beside him.

Marriage was a Christian way of life for them. Marriage, even more than the monastery, could test character. The spouse could show you who you are. Martin recommended marriage for the priests.

The family was for Martin a place to do God's will. The Luther home was a religious institution.

The community in the Augustinian monastery was dwindling. So the Black Cloister was given to the Luthers as a wedding present, and it is known to this day as the Luther House. Student boarders made the family larger, as Katie turned many of the rooms into a kind of boarding house. Festive meals, student meetings, loud debates, and long talks at the dinner table filled the old monastery. The Luther House was seldom recommended to those who sought a quiet place to stay.

In the year of the marriage, 1525, Duke Frederick the Wise died. Luther's political advocate was replaced by an even more loyal friend, Duke John of Saxony. The Turks conquered Hungary. There was warfare in France. The Holy Roman Empire was defending its borders. There was no time for Emperor Charles V to carry out the verdict of the Council of Worms against Luther, and he was safe for a while in these trying times.

Katie and Martin raised five of their six children. Hans was born in 1526. Elizabeth arrived in 1527 and was buried in 1528 in the Wittenberg City Church. Magdalene was born in 1529. She died when she was twelve.

Martin loved Magdalene ("Lenchen") dearly. Perhaps it was because she sang like a bird. Perhaps it was what she'd said to her father about God. She spoke freely and openly with him about faith. He asked if she were ready to go to her Heavenly Father. She was, and Dr. Luther could hardly comprehend her willingness to leave him. He remembered her saying: "You are my earthly father, but God is my heavenly Father."

Luther held her in his arms as she died. He could not understand why he was so torn, for Lenchen was going to be with her Heavenly Father. Yet he longed to keep her on earth in Wittenberg. Lenchen's words were surely a comfort to him. Her faith must have helped old Luther as the enemy of death often gripped him in illness. Martin Luther knew that death would not dance last. Heaven is life.

Eleven foster children made their home at the Luther House. Katie boarded twenty-four students in the many rooms of the

1526

German princes form the Lutheran Federation, called the League of Torgau.

Another annual Imperial Diet is held. All princes attend the Diet of Speyer. Elector John the Steadfast returns to Wittenberg to make Saxony a Lutheran state.

June 7: Hans Luther is born.

Luther writes "Exposition of Jonah."

1527

December 10: Elizabeth Luther is born.

A school and parish visitation, led by Luther, uncovers a great need for educational reform in Saxony. New songs and hymns are created, including "A Mighty Fortress."

The Luther family has become an heroic family. At a gathering in church, school, or home, come to honor and tell about your own living hero. Luther was a folk hero.

Plan a festival combining song, drama, and Luther sayings. This book can be a text for the celebration.

Magdalena (Lenchen) Luther who died at the age of twelve in her father's arms

---

It is very fine when a husband exhibits his good will toward his wife also by his bad manners. On the other hand, it is shameful and scandalous when some men show themselves to be contrary, morose, and bitter toward their wives and neither by their words nor their actions give any indication of love and good will. (Luther)

It is impossible to keep peace between man and woman in family life if they do not condone and overlook each other's faults but watch everything to the smallest point. For who does not at times offend? (Luther)

God lays souls into the lap of married people, souls begotten from their own body, on which they may practice all Christian works. For when they teach their children the Gospel, parents are certainly their apostles, bishops, and ministers. (Luther)

The forgiveness of sins is in all creatures. Not all trees grow straight; not all waters flow straight; nor is the earth level everywhere. Therefore, the statement is true: He who does not know how to close an eye does not know how to rule. (Luther)

Copy something in writing into your journal and show it to someone else.

Close your eyes and hear the singing, laughter, and loud sounds of the large Luther household.

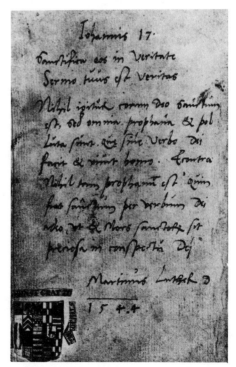

By Martin Luther

Eat an apple or some other fruit in Katie's garden, and reflect on her inspiration for Reformation ministry. Think deeply about how women have led in reform.

1528

Luther's daughter, Elizabeth, dies at the age of one year.

Reformation artists, Durer and Grunewald, die.

1529

December 17: Magdelena Luther is born.

Humanist Erasmus flees the Reformation to Freiburg.

The second Diet is held in Speyer. King Charles V is still at war and sends Ferdinand as representative. Protestant princes vote down endorsing the Edict of Worms against Luther. They are now called Protestants.

Luther writes both the German Large and Small Catechism for educating children through the family.

October: Protestants agree that something has to be done. They hold a preliminary meeting in the Castle of Philip of Hesse to form a political alliance. Zwingli and Luther meet to discuss Holy Communion.

home. The busy sounds were well known to those who had been to the home. The family was a market place of ideas, wonder, song, debate, and love.

Katie managed the chores of the household. Martin did not always agree with her on whether they talked too much. Sometimes he asked her to pray the Lord's Prayer before speaking. Katie sometimes asked Martin to stop talking at mealtime so students could eat their soup, which was turning cold. Students sat spellbound and wrote down most of what he said. These "table talks" often annoyed Dr. Luther. He would on occasion blurt out nonsense and urge them to also write that down. The conversations with students often became loud and rough. Katie helped them (and Martin) to curb their tongues.

Katie's garden was large and beautiful. She made the best sauerkraut, did all the butchering, and brewed the best beer in town, according to Martin.

Martin was often depressed, and Katie was his counselor. She healed him with her sound words and simple faith, as well as with herbs and common medicines. Perhaps the greatest Luther stories were known by Katie and have not been recorded.

The flow of Luther's pen seemed constant. Pamphlets, commentaries, sermons, letters, and songs all poured through the printing presses of Wittenberg. What was the source of inspiration? Much of the warmth and spirit of the writings came from life with Katie and the children. Not only did the family rub off Luther's rough edges, but it warmed his heart and kept his mind and words on the primary concerns of common people. Those who heard him and read his words could understand him, for he was one of them.

The Bible

The Evangelicals, the followers of Luther, focused on the Gospel. Their emphasis lay not so much with sacraments as with Scriptures. Their sights were less on the rules and regulations of the Church than on the Bible. The family was a possible place for the reading of the Word. The Luther family could lead the way for the family Bible.

In 1545, Martin Luther's entire German Bible was ready for printing. The translation was vivid and picturesque. Woodcuts by his friend Cranach made the German Bible even more meaningful. Both the vivid language and the woodcuts gave the people a vision of believing, and faith for many was increased through art.

Vom Himmel Hoch
(From Heaven High)

Over a period of thirty years, Luther preached thousands of sermons and created many pageants. Many of the pageants were based on sermon series preached during Church Year cycles. Some songs were written for his own family. He would stroll as troubadour among the children, strumming his lyre. The most famous of his Christmas songs is "From Heaven High," which first appeared in the Klugsche hymnal of 1535. His love for pageantry with children is evident: If we want to train children we must become childlike with them. In 1535 his own children's ages were nine, six, four, two, and one. Other orphans and relatives living in the Luther House must have been a great cast for the sixteen stanzas to "Vom Himmel Hoch." It is the childlike telling of the story of baby Jesus. This translation by Dr. Roland Bainton shows the childlike spirit of Dr. Luther.

O dear Lord Jesus for your head
Now will I make the softest bed.
The chamber where this bed shall be
Is in my heart inside of me.

I can play the whole day long.
I'll dance and sing for you a song.
A soft and soothing lullaby,
So sweet that you will never cry.

From heaven high I come to earth;
I bring you tidings of great mirth.
This mirth is such a wondrous thing
That I must tell you all and sing.

He is the Christ, our God indeed,
Who saves you all in ev'ry need.
He will Himself your Saviour be,
From all wrongdoing make you free.

Look now, you children, at the sign.
A manger cradle, far from fine,
A tiny Baby you will see;
Upholder of the world is He.

O dear Lord Jesus for your head
Now will I make the softest bed.
The chamber where this bed shall be
Is in my heart inside of me.

Translation by Roland H. Bainton

Vom Himmel hoch da komm ich her

Martin Luther 1539

„Vom Him - mel hoch da komm ich her, ich bring euch gu - te neu - e Mär, der gu - ten Mär bring ich so viel, da - von ich singn und sa - gen will.

The Luther Bible of 1541

1530

Luther is forced back into hiding by Charles V, who has returned to Germany after nine years of absence.

April 15: A Diet is to be held at Augsburg. Luther must be separate from those attending the Diet. He can go no further, for he is under the Imperial ban and will not be safe outside the territory of John the Steadfast. Luther advises the Augsburg Confession writings from Coburg Castle.

While at Coburg Castle, Luther's father Hans dies. Martin grieves that he cannot be with him before his death.

June 25: The Augsburg Confession is read in public as a statement of Protestant faith. Melanchton drafts the main document, with regular advice by Luther from Coburg. Dr. John Eck, who had debated in Leipzig with Luther, is ordered by Charles V to expose any Lutheran errors.

1531

Lutherans draft a defense of the Augsburg Confession.

November 9: Son Martin Luther is born.

Luther's mother, Margaretha, dies.

Protestant dukes and cities create the Schmalkald Federation, a mutual agreement between Evangelical states and cities to serve as a defense pact. Luther is ill and receives guests on the third floor.

Reading the Scriptures was for Martin a great responsibility. It was not to be done thoughtlessly or flippantly. He had studied long and hard, and the Gospel was not yet entirely clear to him. Would the people read the Bible now that it was translated? Would children have the opportunity to see and read it? Could it get into the schools? Martin had been twenty-one before he read his first Bible.

The school seemed to be the best network for reading the German Bible, for it could be used as a text for reading German. Bible and language belonged together. For Luther, the Bible belonged to the curriculum.

Adults needed help to read and understand the Bible. Education was to be a continuous joy for all. Study and learning for Luther was a daily and lifelong privilege. He fought to get both German and the German Bible into the Latin schools of his day. The name of Dr. Luther was well known among educators. He was an important reformer of public education. He saw all education as the right of all people.

The Augsburg Confession

After the Diet of Worms in 1521, the writings of Luther were to be burned and stopped. However, his new writings poured out through the Empire. King Charles V was too busy fighting wars in France, Turkey, and Italy to come to get Luther. Charles could not settle the Civil War and rebellion inside his own Empire until he had made peace with outside enemies. This lasted for most of the rest of Luther's life.

When the wars were done, King Charles could crush the Evangelicals and outlaw the Lutherans. It was 1530, and the Emperor chose to settle the matter in Augsburg. The Lutherans were invited.

The Luther followers prepared a manifesto. Melanchton, a professor at Wittenberg and a close friend of Luther's, masterminded the manifesto.

Luther could not travel to Augsburg, for it lay outside Saxony and Luther was still under arrest. He stayed in the Coburg Castle, not far from Augsburg, and watched the meeting from a distance. Again in a castle, Luther waited, listened, and prayed. He trusted his younger and more diplomatic friend Melanchton. Daily a messenger brought reports to the castle. From there he coached the Evangelicals.

Martin marveled at the soft and sane spirit of Philip Melanchton, and found no word to change in the manifesto. He commended Philip for his peaceful spirit in angry times.

Erhalt Uns, Herr, Bei Deinem Wort
(Lord, Keep Us Steadfast in Your Word)

When in 1541 Germany was in danger of being invaded by Sultan Suleiman and the Turks, Elector Frederick asked pastors to pray for Germany's protection. As a response Luther prepared a service that included the hymn "Lord, Keep Us Steadfast in Your Word." The very first copy translated into English reads as follows:

Lord, keep us in Thy word and work;
Restrain the murderous Pope and Turk,
Who fain would tear off Thy throne
Christ Jesus, Thy beloved Son.

Later, when neither Pope nor Turk seemed to threaten Germany, the text was altered to include enemies in general. The hymn was published in broadsheet at Wittenberg in 1542, and was printed in Low German in Magdeburg. It may be Luther's tune and seems patterned after a plainsong from the twelfth century, which was the stock from which other hymn tunes were taken.

Lord, keep us steadfast in thy word,
Curb those who fain by craft or sword
Would wrest the kingdom from thy Son,
And set at naught all he hath done.

Lord Jesus Christ, thy power make known,
For thou art Lord of lords alone;
Defend thy Christendom, that we
May evermore sing praise to thee.

Erhalt uns, Herr, bei deinem Wort
Altkirchlich / Martin Luther 1543

Er-halt uns, Herr, bei deinem Wort und steu-re dei-ner Fein-de Mord, die Je-sum Chri-stum, dei-nen Sohn, wollen stür-zen von dei-nem Thron.

For twenty-eight years, since I became a doctor, I have now constantly read and preached the Bible; and yet I have not exhausted it but find something new in it every day. (Luther)

Scripture is its own light. It is a fine thing when Scripture explains itself. (Luther)

That the Holy Scriptures cannot be penetrated by study and talent is most certain. Therefore your first duty is to begin to pray, and to pray to this effect that if it please God to accomplish something for His glory—not for yours or any other person's—He very graciously grant you a true understanding of His words. (Luther)

Coburg Castle by Lucas Cranach

Luther publishes his "Warning to His Beloved Germans."

Luther's writings speak of God in the language of common people. In private, he writes poetry and hymns. He is working with others on the German Bible translation.

Dr. Luther lectures in his own dining room, in the spacious forty-room Black Cloister. Even the dinner hour is like an extra class meeting. After his death, students publish 6000 Luther entries from their notebooks as Luther's "Table Talks."

1533

January 28: Paul Luther is born.

1534

Luther and collaborators complete the German Bible translation.

December 17: Margaretha Luther is born.

1536

May: The "Schmalkald Articles" are drawn up.

Erasmus of Rotterdam dies. This great Dutch leader of the Renaissance, who corresponded with Luther, exposed scandal in the Church and did not join either side in the Reformation dispute.

1537

On a trip, Martin Luther becomes very ill and rests in the Augustinian church in Gotha. During the stay he makes out his will. The castle in Gotha contains Cranach paintings.

Dr. Melanchton wanted to make a way for peace and to arbitrate between hostile sides. He hoped the Augsburg Confession, as it came to be known, would be a healing force. But the fractures were not healing in the three months of meeting (April to June in 1530).

Dr. John Eck represented both the Pope and the emperor. His staff and colleagues argued against Melanchton's position. The emperor heard both sides, as the Augsburg Confession was read both in Latin and in German. The reading took over three hours, while all leaned to hear the booming voice of the reader. It is reported that Charles V slept through much of the reading. Having heard the reading, the king declared that Dr. Eck had won and the Evangelicals had lost.

In all of this, King Charles did something significant for the Lutherans. He asked the Pope to look at the issues that had caused the reform. He raised the question: What made for this upheaval within the Church?

Twenty-five years later, there would be a second meeting at Augsburg. It would come ten years after Luther's death and be named the Peace of Augsburg. It opened the way for peace between the Evangelicals and the Roman Catholic Church.

Peace and War

Peace! Peace! was the cry, but there was no peace. The Reformation movement was not in Luther's control. Nor did he wish to control it. Some reforms had gone too far. He argued with them and he warned them.

Many hoped for freedom. Luther had clearly written that peasants and nobles were equal in the sight of God. But human rights were not equal, and there was a clashing of steel and clubs on the horizon.

It was not a time for simple advice. Some used what Luther wrote as an excuse to revolt. He had advocated rights for all people. Rights and power come from the Word and not from the sword. But the sword did come, and the peasants and nobles fought a terrible war.

Luther was blamed and blessed. Some thought he went too far in promoting personal rights. Some blamed him for withdrawing too soon. His sensitive spirit was caught in the midst of the turmoil. There was not time to deal with issues adequately. So much needed counsel and care. He felt helpless, and sometimes rejected and useless.

Quarreling broke out among his supporters. He was often too ill, and finally too old, to become as involved as he ought. He felt guilty for what was happening. What had been so hopeful in the past now seemed so hostile.

The church of God approves articles of faith or the Scriptures as with the endorsement of an inferior, that is, it acknowledges and confesses them as a servant does the seal of his lord. (Luther)

The church is the pupil of Christ, sitting at His feet and hearing His Word so that she may know how to pass judgment on everything, how to serve in one's calling, how to administer public offices, aye, also how to eat, drink, and sleep, that there may be no doubt about the proper conduct in any work of life but, surrounded on all sides by the Word of God, one may constantly walk in joy and in the light. (Luther)

The existence of the church is an article of faith; for it is apprehended by faith, not by sight. (Luther)

What do you hear or see that is like or unlike this saying?

What mood or emotion does this saying evoke in you?

Reflect on the saying—and let it penetrate deep into your mind.

Augsburg where diet took place in 1530

Gelobet Seist Du, Jesu Christ (All Praise to You Eternal Lord)

One stanza of the hymn "All Praise to You Eternal Lord" was a popular pre-Reformation song, and was sung in the vernacular German. On Christmas day, it was sung as the people's response, with the Kyrie Eleison added at the end. So it was called "Leise," or softly. Since the sixteenth century, it has had its present German form. Luther added six stanzas and published it in 1523; it also appeared one year later in the Erfurt Enchiridia. Luther used several sources for creating hymns, such as translations from Latin hymns, psalm poems, verses of the Bible, and revisions of pre-Reformation German hymns. He also wrote many original songs. J. S. Bach used the hymn "All Praise to You Eternal Lord" in Cantatas 64 and 91, and in his Christmas Oratorio.

All praise to thee, Eternal Lord,
Clothed in a garb of flesh and blood;
Choosing a manger for thy throne,
While worlds on worlds are thine alone.

A little child, thou art our guest,
That weary ones in thee may rest;
Forlorn and lowly is thy birth,
That we may rise to heaven from earth.

Gelobet seist du, Jesu Christ
15. Jahrhundert / Wittenberg 1524

Ge-lo-bet seist du, Je-su Christ, daß du

Mensch ge-bo-ren bist von ei-ner

Jung-frau, das ist wahr; des freu-et

sich der En-gel Schar. Ky-ri-e-leis.

1538

Martin Luther writes: "If I should lose my Katie I would not take another wife, though I were offered a queen."

1540

The famed Katherine Portal is built into the Wittenberg Luther House.

1542

A precise listing of Katie's livestock is reported: eight pigs, five cows, nine calves, and chickens, geese, and Tolpel the dog.

1543

Luther publishes the Commentary on Genesis.

1546

January 23: Luther travels to Eisleben for business with sons Martin and Paul. They wait in Halle for the Saale River ice to break so they may cross. He is often called to counsel legal matters. Luther is not well.

Luther counsels the counts. He preaches in St. Andrews Church and organizes a Latin school in Eisleben.

February 17: After three weeks, Luther helps two counts to settle their inheritance argument.

Always Luther hunted for his hope, love, and direction in God's Word. He could not always find his hope and love in the people. Even his own St. Mary's congregation in Wittenberg seemed to lack affection. He grew increasingly impatient and accused them of being loveless and immoral. He left them for a while, so deep was his hurt.

Dr. Luther even grumbled against his students as the counter Reformation grew in strength. Sides and issues were unclear. None were certain about what to do.

Martin Luther complained of being tired and old. He was more than sixty, in a time when the average life span was twenty-eight years.

Katie was gracious throughout and reminded Martin of God's bounty, and of God's own trust in the human race. She kept him in touch with the community of people. Her affection and devotion kept alive Luther's positive theology.

During all these struggling times, Luther kept writing to friends and family. His ink well had not grown dry. His affection insight, and good counsel was replenished daily.

The Final Days

Martin Luther traveled far to do his work. The Reformation was a movement that caused old lines to change. What was once settled was now open for discussion. What had been required for centuries was now an option. It was not easy to be both leader and counselor in the midst of fast-changing times. Congregations made great demands.

He often wrote home for assurance and advice. Katie was sometimes worried by his letters and troubled even more by the problems he kept from her. His letters likewise counseled Katie. She sometimes confessed anxiety, worry, and lack of sleep on his behalf. He begged her to leave the worry to God. Had she not read her Catechism? God would do the worrying and the caring. Half teasing, he pretended she were God, and wondered how she could manage the universe while being so anxious. He meant thereby to reassure her that God would provide.

Martin and Katie dealt with one another as though always under the watchful eye of God. The Luther family seemed always to be truly present before God. They had now lived together in the Black Cloister for twenty years. Luther was not well. It was wintertime. He was not fit to travel. He had an emergency call to come to Eisleben, to settle a property dispute between two counts. He was not fit to travel. But in the winter he went to the town of his birth. Luther heard out their dispute, and it was soon settled. While in Eisleben, Dr. Luther

Aus Tiefer Not Schrei Ich Zu Dir
(From Depths of Woe I Cry to Thee)

The verses of "From Depths of Woe I Cry to Thee" are based on Psalm 130. The song first appeared in 1523 and in the same year was included in the Wittenberg Etlich Christlich Lieder. The four-stanza hymn was later expanded to five stanzas and included in Luther's Christian Songs for Funerals. In 1525, it was sung in the Castle Church at the funeral of Luther's patron and elector, Frederick the Wise. Luther gathered servants around himself in the Coburg Castle during the Diet at Augsburg and found comfort in the hymn. On February 20, 1546, it was sung at a funeral service in Halle while Luther's body was being brought from Eisleben to his home in Wittenberg. The translation by Catherine Winkworth became part of the English chorale book in 1863. Luther possibly wrote the tune. Cantata 38 by J. S. Bach was based on this hymn.

Out of the depths I cry to thee,
O Lord, my sins bewailing!
Bow down thy gracious ear to me,
Make thou my prayer availing.
Mark not my misdeeds in thy book,
But on my sins in mercy look,
Or who can stand before thee?

Like those who watch upon the wall
To welcome in the morning,
My soul doth wait thy quiet call,
Herself with hope adorning.
So may all Israel look for thee,
And in thy day find mercy
And plenteous redemption. Amen.

Luther's last word was an answer to a question about his faith in Christ. He said "Yes." Think of a good last word to say in the journey of faith and life.

All ages can join in making a "roots mural" of Martin Luther and of one another. Label the scribblings or paintings. Make notes, write feelings and ideas, and tell "roots stories" from the mural.

Write simple Luther poems. Make up limericks and ballads, and turn history into a musical event.

Katie's bronze grave plaque in Torgau

February 17: Tonight Luther complains of chest pains. A second attack comes at two A.M. During his third attack, friend and pastor Justus Jonas asks if Luther is willing to die in the name of Jesus. Dr. Martin Luther's final recorded word is a strong "Yes!" He dies at age sixty-two.

February 18: There is a funeral at St. Andrews, Eisleben. The tin coffin box rides on a horsedrawn wagon in a procession back to Wittenberg. The procession carries Luther's body through the Castle Church door on which he nailed the ninety-five theses thirty years before. His body is laid to rest into a crypt in the floor before the pulpit.

1547

Lucas Cranach the Elder paints an altar triptych that can now be seen in the City Church of Wittenberg.

1550

Katie Luther moves to her farm at Wachsdorf. In wartime, she and her family are forced to move to Magdeburg. She worked both the farm and the Cloister.

December 20, 1550: Katherine dies and is buried at St. Mary's, the City Church of Torgau. Her life was a journey of faith.-

drew up plans to begin a school there. He was a pioneer of education even until the end. He also took time to preach in the city church.

On this visit Martin had a severe gall bladder attack. Katie was worried and glad Hans, who was now twenty, was with his father.

Martin wrote to Katie asking her not to worry. He told her that God was his Protector. The peace of God was his power to overcome fear. This protection was greater than what she or all the angels could give. Finally, Luther spoke of the Protector as the Christ, born of Mary in the manger and now seated beside God. This Christ, at woman's breast and Father's side, gave Martin his rest.

Martin Luther died at night in Eisleben, just as he'd been born at night in this same town, sixty-two years earlier.

A death mask of his face and hands was cast. All Germany began to mourn. A parade carried his body home through Halle into Wittenberg. People stood in tribute; bells rang in honor. Some said that Elijah had now gone home, and that horsemen with chariots had come to take him. The mantle of the prophet was now on them.

The circle of rippling water, of his baptism, had encircled him from the beginning. From the first day Martin was in Christ. All his life he'd sought the meaning of this miracle of salvation. He found grace in God's great picture book: the Bible. And when he found it there, he was not content until he had told it and translated it into the language of the German people. All were to know the life inside that circle of Christ.

Under the tree outside Erfurt, at age twenty-one, he'd trembled before God. He trembled at the first Mass in the Augustinian cloister of Erfurt. But he did not tremble at age sixty-two. He rested. The trembling was gone and the trust was there. Christ made the difference. The Christ picture revealed in the Scriptures cast out the fear.

The right to trust God is for all who journey in faith.

Ein Feste Burg Ist Unser Gott
(A Mighty Fortress Is Our God)

We do not know the exact occasion for which the hymn "A Mighty Fortress" was written. Perhaps it was created in 1529 for the Diet of Spires. At this Council the German princes protested against restrictions on their liberties, and they were named Protestants. The imagery for this hymn based on Psalm 46 was formed in Wartburg Castle. This great hymn interprets Psalm 46 into the time and struggle of Luther's Germany.

The hymn was one of the very great hymns of the Church and spread rapidly through Germany. It is reported that Luther sang it daily at Coburg. Other reformers reportedly were comforted during banishment while hearing the hymn sung by a little girl at Weimar. Gustavus Adolphus had it sung by his army before the Battle of Leipzig in 1631. For immigrants it has been a traveling hymn.

It was already translated into English by Coverdale in 1539. By 1900 the hymn had been made into over eighty translations in fifty-three languages. Today it can be sung in 200 tongues, including 63 versions in English.

Frederick the Wise spoke of it as God Almighty's grenadier march. Carlyle heard in this hymn the first murmur of earthquakes and the sound of Alpine avalanches. "A Mighty Fortress" formed the base for J. S. Bach's Cantata 80.

Luther's death

A mighty fortress is our God,
A bulwark never failing;
Our helper he amid the flood
Of mortal ills prevailing:
For still our ancient foe
Doth seek to work us woe;
His craft and power are great,
And, armed with cruel hate,
On earth is not his equal.

Did we in our own strength confide
Our striving would be losing;
Were not the right Man on our side,
The Man of God's own choosing.
Dost ask who that may be?
Christ Jesus, it is he;
Lord Sabaoth his Name,
From age to age the same,
And he must win the battle.

Luther Dramas

Instructions

The Luther Dramas can be used in many ways. They may be read responsively, performed as a reading theater, spoken as devotions, read during worship, staged as a Luther play, or studied as a lesson. They may be read on location at appropriate times on a journey or staged as scenes within a Luther festival. Use them to close a day, open a discussion, or guide prayer. Read them quietly by candlelight, or combine them with lighting and music. There are many ways to share in the excitement of drama.

Birth

Setting: This setting contains a clock, a crib, a font, and a candle.

A: It's Eisleben in Saxony. At night.

B: The village clock has struck 11 P.M. There's a light in the window.

A: It's a boy. Their first son.

B: Hans Luder has big plans for the child. He will not be poor. He will learn Latin as soon as possible and live like a lawyer or doctor.

A: Margaretha, his mother, has stories from old Eisenach to tell him. She has wisdom and piety for the little one's spirit.

B: They are filled with fear and hope at once. It is a time of poverty, and the Black Plague is doing a death dance through the land.

A: Like others, they hope the newborn will live. They now have two. They will have others.

B: Some will live.

A: And take care of them in their old age. The old also have need of daily food.

B: It was almost midnight when it happened.

A: Hans washed the copper dust of the mines off his hands so he could help Margaretha.

B: In the morning Hans took the son up the hill, to the church of St. Peter and St. Paul.

A: A three-minute walk.

B: To be baptized by the priest. It was the three of them: the priest, the child, and Hans.

A: On St. Martin's Day, the Saint of Tours.

B: And so his name would be Martin Luder, or Luther.

A: It was a small chapel inside a fortress tower.

B: Both were round: the font and the fortress.

A: The tower was a chapel and fortress at once.

B: A watch tower against the enemy.

A: A fortress is a place for a font.

B: Baptism would be a stronghold for Martin.

A: A strength. A tower.

B: Baptism gave Luther an armor, a protection. It was his defense.

A: When severely tempted, he could say: "I am baptized."

B: He would live to say it to Satan: "I am baptized."

A: Baptism was Martin's weapon. Christ's name on him.

B: Now he was Christ's. He wanted Satan to know that.

A: He wanted to know for sure: Martin belongs to Christ.

B: To say it was his power.

A: To sing it.

B: To pray it.

A: To know it. He was it.

B: The name of Jesus Christ was his stronghold.

A: The name circled him, like the font.

B: Like the fortress.

A: He lived inside the strong name of Jesus.

B: Christ was on his mind, in his prayers.

A: And around him, on every side.

B: A fortress. And a moat around it.

The Middle Ages

Setting: This setting includes a painter with easel and painting materials. An artist is on location painting or exhibiting a painting throughout the dialogue. Old maps, charts, or artifacts may depict the time: the Middle Ages. Character B is the painter; character A is the observer or critic. Each color and brush mark has a symbolic meaning that describes the Middle Ages. A towel and wash basin filled with water are at hand.

A: What are you painting?

B: The Middle Ages. I'm titling it: "One Thousand Years." *(Writes title.)*

A: Is that how long it lasted? The Middle Ages?

B: I think so. I'm starting with a dab or orange.

A: What does the orange mean?

B: It stands for Christ. He is like the liveliness of orange—to me. The divine one. *(Begins to add blue.)* And now a little blue.

A: What does the blue mean?

B: I'm adding some blue to the orange. It's for his humanity.

A: It's turning green.

B: It was a good time; a green time. The five hundred years after Christ's birth was a bright green time. *(Begins to add red.)* And now the red.

A: What is the red you're adding?

B: The Apostles; the Church Fathers. They formed the Faith. They held councils to choose the books of the Bible. Some kept the Faith by giving up their lives.

A: Martyrs?

B: Sometimes. You see it's turning brown. *(Colors mix into dark brown.)* It's for the monks and the priests who preached Christ to all of Europe. *(Brushes brown on many parts of canvas.)* They were everywhere.

A: Why are you marking all over the canvas?

B: That's why. They were everywhere. Around 300 and 400 A.D. the monks and priests won all Europe for Rome. Rome was headquarters of the Church.

A: You're painting a cross.

B: Rome is where I'm painting this bold sign of the cross. In red and blue, in honor of Paul and Peter who came to Rome. It's the place of stones and catacombs, and creeds.

A: You seem to be having fun with all the colors. It looks joyful. You're adding bright orange.

B: Lots of orange.

A: It's Christlike. A living color.

B: Now I'm bringing in another color: purple. *(Adds purple.)*

A: It's strong. Daring.

B: It's for the Mohammedans. I'm painting near the edge of the canvas: to the far right, to the East. *(Makes swirls with paint.)*

A: It looks like a whirlwind.

B: It's like a birth. Multitudes are emerging in Arabia. *(Sprinkles sand on canvas.)* See, I'm mixing sand with the purple paint. *(Begins to add blue.)*

A: And you're adding some blue-green.

B: It's for the Mediterranean Sea. The Mohammedans emerged all along the Sea. *(Begins white crosses.)* Even into the Holy Land.

A: What is the year?

B: 1000 A.D.

A: What do these white crosses signify?

B: This was the time of the Crusades. It is marking where many Christians died, trying to reclaim the grave and birthplace of Jesus from Mohammedans. *(Makes tiny crosses.)*

A: Why these very tiny crosses?

B: For the Children's Crusade. Many children died along the way. *(Starts to add white to big cross.)*

A: You're adding white to the big cross of Rome.

B: Rome was now the proud capital of Christendom, and also of the Holy Roman Empire. Both the Pope and the Emperor were there. *(Adds some blue to cross.)*

A: And the white in Rome?

B: The Crusades began from there. The Pilgrims always went with a blessing.

A: What is the warm blue you are adding to the Rome cross?

B: It's where the Pope is. Pope means Papa. *(Adds lots of blue.)*

A: You are making the Roman cross larger. It's starting to cover the canvas.

B: The authority and the power of the Pope grew. The control of the Church went out from Rome.

A: Now the white has spread throughout the canvas. The original white of Rome is moving like a lava flow.

B: It's the authority from the capital city. *(Paints furiously, beginning to use all colors.)*

A: You're sweating. You're painting harder. All the colors are merging.

B: I am painting the so-called Holy Inquisition: the witchhunt. Many were killed in the name of Jesus.

A: What does that mean?

B: Some in the Church used Jesus as their excuse for power, even to put to death those who disagreed. *(Adds much yellow and red.)* I need more yellow and red.

A: Is the yellow the Inquisition?

B: It's the many fires that burned people at stakes. *(Marks the initials JH.)* I'll mark JH in the fire.

A: Whose initials?

B: John Huss, the Bohemian, who was burned 100 years before Luther lived.

A: He was a witch?

B: He was a devout Christian. *(Marks ML, and draws large mountain peaks of purple.)* See these mountain peaks, and ML.

A: ML must stand for Martin Luther. And what are the peaks?

B: This is where the monks lived: in the high mountains; in the caves.

A: Alone?

B: Often alone. Some were together, in silence. Some single. Others in monasteries.

A: It's hard to find where this whole painting began: the first brush of orange, for Christ; and the cross of red, for the Apostles.

B: It's in there.

A: It's become so complicated.

B: By the year 1500 there were so many ways to see salvation. *(Paints a white strip down the center.)* I need enough white to finish this line down the center.

A: You seem to be placing something very simple through the middle of everything.

B: It's a white cloth: a towel. The Church needed a simple towel.

A: A towel?

B: To learn what it means to serve one another. To find Christ in the neighbor. All they needed was a towel.

A: It still looks so complex. The painting has so many parts.

B: Luther saw the times to be that way. He kept looking until he found the towel. You know the monogram JC. It belongs on the towel. *(Labels JC monogram on towel.)*

A: Where was the towel? Was it hidden?

B: In the hand of Christ.

A: Just a towel? Is that what Luther found?

B: And some water; and each other. *(While B cleans brushes, A washes feet of B or others.)*

Monasteries

Setting: Character B has set up an exhibit of sketches and drawings; Character A comes to look at the exhibit. The drawings are an aid to understanding the origin of monasteries and the desire of persons to be saved.

A: Are these your sketches?

B: I drew them. The exhibit has a theme.

A: Let me guess the theme: "Mansions." Those look like many mansions.

B: I call it: "What Must I Do to Be Saved?"

A: But they're drawings of buildings.

B: Places of long ago—in the desert where people went to find salvation.

A: Here's a drawing of a cave. A dugout. It's quiet.

B: Alone. It's like this other one on a high rock. Alone.

A: Looks like a hiding place.

B: It was a hiding place. All of these were types of hiding places for a thousand years. Like hermits, they lived in caves and on top of rock pillars. Isolated. Set apart.

A: A weekend retreat.

B: For always. A lifetime retreat. When some went up, they never again came down. The only way to get something such as food to the top of this colony was by the rope.

A: They must have had a reason.

B: To please God. They hoped God would approve of their life.

A: Did they suffer?

B: On purpose. They believed it would atone for their sins. They were called hermits.

A: It makes me think of the hermit crab—in the shell.

B: They lived in that simple place. This was a way for them to have eternal life—by leaving this world behind.

A: But they were still in this world: in the desert; on the high rock.

B: They turned inward. They lived in the spirit. They showed God the heart, in prayers. They were naked before God. They were stripped of all earthly possessions.

A: Short of death.

B: Atoning for sins, this way; while others lived in regular houses.

A: These look like monasteries.

B: Each had his own cell.

A: A cottage.

B: There they prayed, meditated, kept vigil. Otherwise they worked.

A: The cells look barren.

B: They owned no property, not even a book, a pen, or a piece of paper.

A: They gave up everything.

B: Whatever they needed was given them by the one in charge: the abbot, the father.

A: You drew this building so far away from any other.

B: It was away from others. Those who lived there were called monks. They would never visit their parents, would never get married, never buy anything, and never go home.

A: You seem to have many of these sketches named "Monasteries."

B: Thousands were built between 500 and 1500 A.D. throughout Europe, from Spain to England.

A: I can't read your writing.

B: It's in Latin. It's a list of things to do and not do. Rules.

A: Rules?

B: Each organization or household was under some rule written by some saint. The rule instructed them in every way.

A: What order was this?

B: Benedictine, after the Order of St. Benedict.

A: And this one?

B: There were such orders as Franciscan, Dominican, and Augustinian. They were each under the supervision of an abbot. Abbot means papa, Abba.

A: Was there a mother?

B: The monasteries for women were known as convents. The director was called Mother Superior.

A: What did the abbot do?

B: He had absolute power, complete control. No one could complain or find fault against him.

A: Did the monks get along?

B: There was no rank among them.

A: What was their work?

B: They worked in fields and gardens; some built churches and monasteries. They were craftsmen: they made pictures and created tools. Some copies books.

A: They weren't just ministers. They did what everyone does.

B: They looked after the poor and needy. They did welfare work.

A: Many begged in behalf of those who had nothing. They were advocates for the poor.

B: Most of all, they showed those around them how to love. They believed it's better to love than to hate. Better to forgive than to fight.

A: You also have sketches of ruins.

B: Over the years some monks became careless about their lives. Many orders closed.

A: Lost their charm?

B: They lost their calling. Some became bad places for anyone to live.

A: Why did you frame this one?

B: It is the monastery in Erfurt of the Augustinian order, where Martin Luther became a priest.

A: St. Augustine inspired the order.

B: It was a strict order. A hermit house. Luther chose it on purpose.

A: I see you have titled it.

B: It's the one that gave me the theme for the exhibit: "What Must I Do to Be Saved?"

A: That makes sense.

B: It's still the people's question.

A: What must I do to be saved?

A Mighty Fortress

Setting: A lyre or guitar placed beside a hymnal can create atmosphere. Live or recorded medieval instrumentation leading into "A Mighty Fortress" will greatly increase the drama.

A: A mighty fortress is our God.

B: What a picture of God: a mighty fortress.

A: Luther lived in a time and land of fortresses.

B: Wartburg castle was a fortress.

A: Five hundred years old when he was a boy.

B: Martin came to Eisenach when he was fourteen. He lived for three years in the Cotta home. It was his high school years.

A: And Wartburg was just up the mountain.

B: He did not go there in those three years, that we know. But there it was: a bastion, a military defense for the territory of Thuringia.

A: A fortress.

B: Part of it was a cultural center. Musicians met there in the Sangersaal (the singing hall) for music festivals.

A: He loved little Eisenach. The castle was at the edge, high in the woods.

B: Martin knew it was there. Twenty years later, friends would kidnap him ten miles outside Eisenach and hurry him at night into this fortress.

A: It was a fortress. A trusty shield. A weapon, of sorts. A defense weapon, one might say.

B: It was not the only castle in his life. More than 900 dotted the countryside of his home territory of Saxony.

A: And there were other fortresses: the cathedrals.

B: In Martin's day the cathedrals had very large and high doors. And there were smaller doors set within the high ones.

A: For the people.

B: And the wide and high doors were for the horses and the military equipment. The cathedral could house an army. Its high and heavy walls were also a fortress.

A: Sometimes the baptistry was a lookout tower. The bells were signals.

B: It was a fortress for the soldiers.

A: And more often a shelter or shield for the town citizens. In times of siege the citizens moved what they needed for survival through the high cathedral gates, into the safety of the twenty-foot thick walls.

B: For Martin Luther, God was a fortress.

A: A fortress for the people.

B: Imagine, the people and animals in the naves, between the statues and crucifixes and beneath the majestic organs.

A: Eating and sleeping beside the ornate pillars and engraved grave plaques.

B: The symbols of God were all around, and between, and underneath.

A: And above.

B: God's house was a fortress.

A: The people would know the picture by heart: A mighty fortress is our God.

B: What a vivid picture.

A: Martin wanted them to see it with their own eyes. He knew they could imagine it, out of their own experience.

B: God is a shield, a bulwark, and a strength.

A: I think they saw the picture.

B: I think I can see it, and I wasn't even there.

A: A mighty fortress is our God.

Believers

Setting: This setting features a display of books on mathematics, prayer, and faith, all mixed together. This drama is about the connection between fact and faith. The atmosphere could look like a science and prayer place at the same time.

Another fitting scene would be a manger with straw.

A: One plus one is two. That's logic.

B: Logic is when something makes sense.

A: It follows a plan of thinking. Logic is order.

B: It's systematic. It's a way of proving.

A: Luther was logical.

B: He was a philosopher. That's what he taught at the University of Wittenberg. He knew the rules for thinking.

A: Reason, they called it.

B: He urged the people to reason.

A: And to believe. He was most of all a believer.

B: Luther knew that faith does not always follow reason.

A: Believing doesn't always follow the rules of logic.

B: Martin said that if God claimed that two and five were eight, he would believe it.

A: And at Worms, at the Emperor's council meeting, he said he could not recant, or reject, his own writing unless he was convinced by conscience and by reason.

B: So he did believe in reason.

A: And the conscience. He thought that God and faith were beyond reason.

B: A person cannot by nature grasp the truths of almighty God.

A: Like what?

B: Like stooping to lie in the feed box of a donkey.

A: That isn't reasonable.

B: And Martin Luther said he could not grasp that in Christ God would stoop to be a derelict on the cross.

A: That isn't reasonable either. But it is part of our true story.

B: That is what Luther believed, and said.

A: It is beyond reason.

B: God in the feed box of a donkey.

A: That's not reasonable.

B: It's believable. It's outside of reason.

A: I see.

B: And believe.

Baptism

Setting: The scene features a place for bathing a baby. Add a baptism sign, such as a font, a cross, and a candle.

A: What are you doing?

B: Giving the baby a bath.

A: In public? In front of all these people?

B: That's why they came. To see it happen.

A: But why here?

B: It's healthy to do it this way. Good for the baby.

A: Healthy for the baby?

B: And wholesome. Whole and holy. It's healthy for all the people. This is a public bath.

A: But they won't all take a bath.

B: They'll join the baby, in a way. See them staring.

A: I've heard of public baths in the Orient.

B: This is the way we have always done it. We bathe the baby when all the people are present.

A: Is the baby really in need of this bath?

B: Very much. The bath is carefully prescribed. The minister has been trained to do it. We follow directions closely.

A: But most anyone knows how to bathe a baby.

B: This is a bath of regeneration, a bath of rebirth.

A: You mean it's not just to clean the baby's skin.

B: It is to clean the baby. The whole baby, for life.

A: Clean as new?

B: Reborn. This is a second birth.

A: You call it a washing.

B: That's how a baby is born. It is washed onto shore through its mother.

A: You mean the birth pangs are like waves that bring the baby to shore?

B: The delivery washes the baby up on dry land. Into the world. Out here with us. On land.

A: But isn't that birth enough? Why this next one?

B: There's more to life than being born. There's living in it.

A: So this is the second birth.

B: It's the life all the people came to share in.

A: They are staring.

B: Of course. It's their imagination that causes them to stare.

A: What do they see? They seem to be looking beyond this place.

B: They see being born again. They recognize it. It happens to them every day.

A: They come here every day to do this.

B: They come here sometimes to practice, so they can do it every day.

A: Continuously?

B: Again and again.

A: Couldn't all this happen at the first birth? With the water from the mother? Couldn't they combine the baptism with the birth?

B: It all gets connected, when you think about it. It did say that this is a rebirth. The first birth is part of the whole picture.

A: One is a creation picture.

B: They both are. And this is a salvation picture. That's the picture in the people's eyes. All the salvation pictures are coming into their eyes.

A: Are there many?

B: The flood, the Red Sea, the story of Jonah, and the burial of Christ. These are flood pictures.

A: And salvation.

B: So that's what they're staring at, the baby's new life. And their own. The baby's new life reminds them of their own.

A: The baby is the object of it all.

B: The subject. The baby will soon learn to stare with this imagination.

A: At what?

B: At whom. At God. At what God does through creation and salvation.

A: You mean, what God is doing right now.

B: All the time. Every day.

A: Continuously.

B: The spirit and the water are always in action.

A: Connection.

B: Both are the language of God. The water and the spirit are how God talks to the baby.

A: The baby needed it.

B: We all need it. We need the baby.

A: It's clear now: We all need the baby.

Translation

Setting: This setting combines the language of the common people with the writings in the Bible. Display the Bible along with other daily sources of communication such as magazines, newspapers, a dictionary, a radio, a tape player.

A: He knew the language of the people.

B: He should. He was born there.

A: I mean, the spirit of their words. It wasn't just a word-for-word translation.

B: More thoughtful than that. Thought by thought, not just word by word.

A: Picture by picture. He said that God talks in pictures. He looked at the people's picture language.

B: Martin Luther felt the spirit of German.

A: That's the way any language is. It has a spirit.

B: He was putting Hebrew and Greek into German images.

A: He was imaginative in his translation.

B: He was being true. It was almost as though Jesus was born in a German cow barn, and Mary was a Saxon maiden.

A: It was more like it all took place in a German village. In their midst.

B: For them.

A: For us it might be more like a birth in a roadside motel.

B: With a parking lot that's filled on a crowded night. And bands going full force.

A: For Luther it was a cow stall.

B: That's the way his friends painted it, with the rolling hills and a German castle in the background.

A: The shepherds were like farmers. The wise men sometimes looked like professors. German professors.

B: Mary was a plump peasant girl from Saxony. And Jesus a husky German boy.

A: Martin enjoyed his Bible that way. The texts had to look like something the people could imagine.

B: He was a master of language. A craftsman.

A: There were many dialects in Germany. Students at the University of Wittenberg came from everywhere. They needed a common German. One the whole nation could read and write and use.

B: He created a German grammar and vocabulary they could all use. He found it by listening to them.

A: He borrowed from them.

B: It came to be known as high German.

A: Merchants, bankers, and professors all used it.

B: It was the German for commerce, education, and legal work.

A: For poetry and literature. For the songs.

B: He was a kind of Daniel Webster.

A: It all came from the people. He collected it. He was the editor of it.

B: It came from their lips and regions.

A: From their eyes, the way they saw.

B: It showed their spirit.

A: Every language has spirit, the spirit of the people.

B: The gospel will find that spirit.

A: That is what Martin knew. He translated the Scriptures into the spirit of German.

B: The spirit had flesh and was alive. The words rang true.

A: In German.

B: It's the same for us. The words look for the spirit.

A: The Gospel will do that in every nation. It will find the people's spirit.

B: And their pictures. Their tone of voice. Their inflections.

A: It's not just words.

B: It gets into their world. Their spirit world. Their life.

A: And transforms their spirit.

B: Into a holy spirit.

A: It transforms their imagination.

B: Into the images of God.

A: No wonder Luther translated the words to read: liebe Maria (dearest Mary).

B: Of course. It's what any good German angel would have whispered.

Beggars

Setting: This scene should show signs of poverty alongside a loaf of bread. At the end of the reading, break and distribute the bread.

A: The reformation was compassionate.

B: Lovers were on the move.

A: Lovers of beggars.

B: Lovers of the poor.

A: Lovers of the neighbor.

B: Martin was such a compassionate person. A lover to the poor.

A: He often said that his roots were with the peasantry, and that is where his father Hans came from.

B: Martin helped write social reforms.

A: Rules and rights for workers.

B: Guidelines against begging.

A: He wrote and published manifestos for nobles about human rights.

B: Some were lengthy pamphlets. One of his flyers was titled "Appeal to the Christian Nobility of the German Nation."

A: He was troubled by the many who took up begging in Wittenberg.

B: Some had to. Some were professionals.

A: He was glad to leave Wartburg, being disguised as Junker Georg. There was much to do in his town of Wittenberg.

B: There was a childhood compassion inside Martin. At Magdeburg, when he was twelve, he'd seen the prince of Anhalt turn into a beggar. This nobleman who chose begging for life made a difference in Martin's spirit.

A: Deep inside the Saxon boy there stirred a heart of pity for all who cried for mercy.

B: He developed an open heart for the underdog.

A: He had an eye for humanity. He felt the pain of those under the heel of power systems. He saw the serfs. He admired the butcher and the maid.

B: He saw the gilded altars, while on their expansive doorsteps many knelt to beg for pence or bread.

A: Statues were overlaid with pure gold and clad in bronze. Those outside who knelt were in rags and bones.

B: Spires reached into the clouds, and their crosses were the highest signs in the city.

A: While spires lifted higher and higher, the citizens bowed lower and lower.

B: The need seemed greater and greater. The unrest increased.

A: The forgiveness was too expensive for some to ever pay.

B: They were in debt for years to come. They were in debt beyond death.

A: Fear gripped the hungry.

B: Hatred welled up in them.

A: They waited for a moment of revenge.

B: If they could ever speak out of their own free will, and with their imagination, they would surely lash out in a revolution.

A: They stood at the edge of reverence and of revolt.

B: They were in need of good laws, justice, and righteousness.

A: Martin sought good ordinances for the workers in the city of Wittenberg.

B: It provided means and encouragement for all kinds in need.

A: There was need for interest-free loans to poor artisans and merchants.

B: New laws set many people's hearts aright.

A: Some walked again was though they counted.

B: It was a time when humankind had lost sight of self-worth.

A: Humanists met in almost every cafe, to drink and to talk about human and civil rights.

B: Martin Luther knew their concerns. He tested any thought that had compassion in it.

A: It was a time of renaissance in some parts of that world.

B: Old masters were being read, and human worth was reconsidered.

A: Some read and took heart. Old poems and paintings reminded people of their worth and rights.

B: Renewal was in the air.

A: And Martin Luther was in the Word asking: Who am I to God?

B: The nation of beggars and castles needed a crier.

A: Martin was the crier. He remembered the begging prince from Anhalt. And the Kyrie out of the mouth of the beggar along the Jericho highway.

B: To be Christ to that beggar is what Martin was called to do.

A: He did it. And that was a word from the Lord.

B: Compassion was hammered out in the rules of righteousness. Justice insists on compassion.

A: Martin found compassion inside justice. He found this mercy in Christ.

B: "We are all beggars."

A: Some believe it was Martin's last saying.

B: Everything we have is given to us.

Prayer Circle

Setting: This setting includes a simple plate of food. The dialogue can take place there.

A: Is that prayer?

B: I didn't know you were looking.

A: Is that how you pray?

B: I don't usually do it this way. I just wanted to be more physical about it this time. More human.

A: All you did was make a circle with your hand over the food.

B: And I signed it with a cross, and said Amen.

A: Were you making fun of prayer?

B: No. I didn't know anyone was looking.

A: Did Luther do that?

B: I don't know. But his prayers feel like that.

A: Like a circle?

B: Like something in close, in front of you. Something physical, specific, real. You can almost see what he's praying about.

A: Your food is getting cold.

B: This food is very important to me. It's here. I wanted to get it into the prayer. So I circled it.

A: That's how Martin prayed?

B: I think I would have done it anyway. To taste it, smell it, and enjoy it always makes me say "Thanks."

A: So he wrote and prayed that way?

B: Martin did it in his hymns. They were as real as life. As though he was there, on location.

A: That's how praying is supposed to be.

B: It's how we prayed when we were little. We named the people. We listed the toys and the things we did by name. We blessed all we could see in our world.

A: And put it into a circle.

B: The circle seemed so big then, and so close. It was right before our eyes.

A: And praying was quite like making the sign of the cross over it all.

B: And we'd hold the toys tighter, as we mentioned them by name. Or looked right at Mother or Father as we told God to bless them. It was all so close.

A: Where do you think Martin learned to pray that way?

B: At home. It was a pious place. And then later from the psalmists.

A: He loved the psalms?

B: It was his prayer book. That's where he thought he found Christ.

A: Where did he find him?

B: In Psalm 22. Crying out the words of the cross.

A: That helped Martin to get in touch with reality?

B: From then on Martin knew that God understood Martin. God's own son felt the way Martin so often felt. That's when God and Martin got very close together.

A: In the psalm.

B: In Jesus, who spoke some of the psalm from the cross.

A: The words of the psalmist.

B: And they were Martin's words. That's the miracle. That the words of the psalmist, Jesus, and Martin were the same Word.

A: All in the same circle.

Body of Christ

Setting: Include a Holy Communion arrangement. It could be a painting of the Last Supper. It may be a piece of bread and a candle. Be prepared to distribute the bread and to read Luther's sayings about Communion.

A: The Body of Christ.

B: That's what they usually say.

A: The blood of Christ.

B: That's what you usually hear when you come to the Communion table.

A: Sometimes the ministers say Bible verses while we eat and drink.

B: Sometimes they say: "Take and drink. This is the blood of the new covenant."

A: Mostly they say: "The body of Christ. The blood of Christ."

B: That's what you hear, over and over.

A: Four words: The body of Christ. Sometimes it's enough. You don't want them to say more.

B: I know. Sometimes I like to hear the words: "Given for you." Given for you. Given for you.

A: Over and over. Makes it seem like a gift. Given. Only a gift.

B: Or it can sound like: "Given up for you." Given up for you. Christ gave up his life.

A: He didn't hold it back. He sacrificed.

B: For you. For you. For you. That's something to think about. For you.

A: For me. Over and over, for each person.

B: And for each day, each week, each hour, each life.

A: Year after year after year, for you, for you, for me, for me.

B: These few words at Holy Communion are really something.

A: They never seem to quit having new meaning.

B: The blood of Christ. The blood of Christ.

A: That's where the people thought life was. In the blood. There is the life.

B: The life of Christ. The life of Christ.

A: Of Christ. Of Christ. That's closer than from Christ, or with Christ.

B: Of Christ. That's close. Of is close. Like I am of my mother, of my father, of my history.

A: In the creed we say that Jesus is God of God. God of God.

B: Light of light, light of light.

A: It's intimate. Personal. Close relationship.

B: Close as a relative.

A: Family. Body.

B: It's right where we began. Body.

A: Body of Christ. We receive it and we're in it.

B: We're it. The Body of Christ.

Wild Boar

Setting: Arrange a setting to contrast something violent and something gentle. It could be a weapon placed alongside a bowl of grapes.

At the end of the drama everyone may share in eating the grapes.

A: They called him a "wild boar."

B: Sounds like a football tackle or a Saturday night wrestler.

A: It was Martin Luther whom they called a wild boar. Pope Leo X sent the message.

B: A strong name.

A: It was no compliment. Wild boars ravaged the medieval gardens and played havoc on vineyards.

B: The boars could not be contained. They went where they wanted to go. They could not be stopped.

A: They could root their way in, under, and through.

B: The Pope did not feel kindly toward this young monk.

A: Martin made the church leaders uncomfortable. They were not sure where he would pop up next to plague their church councils.

B: Martin pushed and prodded and teased and challenged. He was a restless one.

A: He never quit pressing the church office.

B: He was always pressing a point that he considered a weak point. He had an eye for them.

A: He seemed wild to those who did not appreciate his insight. He had found an inner freedom in the Scriptures, and it compelled him like an inner drive.

B: It seemed to some that he was on a rampage, and none knew if he might soon come running through their garden.

A: He was serious, wreckless, devout.

B: He found the Spirit in the Scriptures.

A: There he met the wild ones before him: Moses and Joseph and Ruth and Rahab and Paul. The wild boars of the Scriptures.

B: And the Apostles.

A: And Jesus. He devastated the hierarchy around him.

B: On the loose. Sure. Driven.

A: Called.

B: He could be captured, bound, held, and burned at any moment.

A: Martin had already wrestled barefisted with God. He knew the spirit of the wild boar.

B: He knew the lamenting and begging and wrestling of others like himself in the psalms.

A: He heard Paul cut to the heart of congregations in Corinth and Galatia. Paul did not pull back. His words were quick. He rushed into their lives.

B: There were many quiet and protected gardens in Martin's time.

A: A wild boar would seem awesome and fierce tearing through their silence, and breaking their vines and branches.

B: There was something to be wild about. Angry about.

A: The fences were high. The common people were often kept silent.

B: In ignorance. By force. Locked into systems.

A: A wild boar in this medieval matrix would be a picture of wildness.

B: To be controlled if possible. At any cost. To capture the wild boar was the edict.

A: Many vineyards were lethargic, trapped, passive. There were moats around the congregations.

B: They were under dominion.

A: In June of 1520 Pope Leo wrote a document, a papal bull, denouncing Martin, comparing him to a serpent spreading poison through heresies.

B: Now the serpent had become a wild boar.

A: The cry went out: A wild boar is loose in the vineyard!

B: Whose vineyard was it?

A: Some of the boars had been caught and burned on the spot.

B: In 1415 such a boar had been burned: John Huss.

A: Luther the boar had plunged into the vineyards with all his might.

B: A streak of energy. A dynamo. Power. Spirit.

A: His spirit ripped open silent places.

B: His words were like fierce grunts to some.

A: He ripped into places of oppression.

B: There was the feel of death in the air.

A: The sounds of his words echoed throughout the Holy Roman Empire.

B: Pamphlets rushed through presses and into the mails across Europe.

A: Sleepy hollows awoke in the Holy Roman Empire.

B: Martin wakened some who had fallen into a deep sleep.

A: There was a wild spirit on the loose.

B: God had loosed a captive, and there was no keeping the preacher silent.

A: The vineyard was wide awake.

B: Some tender branches were broken.

A: Old vines were pruned.

B: The vineyard was reawakened.

Limericks

Setting: This setting could feature a list of rhyming words to depict the concept of writing poems. A few books of poems and limericks can focus the attention on a poetic and playful spirit. Character A sits at a table writing.

A: What are you writing?

B: Limericks about the Pope in Luther's day.

A: To poke fun?

B: No. To tell a piece of history. Facts can be described in rhyme.

A: It feels like a limerick.

B: Tell me one. See if I can find the facts.

A: The Pope had position and power;
  Both Church and the Empire did cower.
  The armies obeyed,
  The kings were afraid;
  His might reached as tall as a tower.

B: How did he get the power?

A: It came slowly. Missionaries taught that the Pope represented Christ. To disobey him was to disobey God.

B: That's power.

A: Then the people were instructed that they could not go to heaven if they were members of the Pope's church.

B: If you weren't a member you would go to hell.

A: Not to believe this was a deadly sin. The Pope had the power to cut off membership.

B: Like the branch of a tree.

A: To be cut off, excommunicated, was the image of terror for the people. It meant hell forever.

B: Tell me in a limerick.

A: Behave and do not rebel,
  For the Pope has the power to sell,
  Your body and soul
  In a fiery hole
  Where you'll burn forever in hell.

B: It's a frightful image. A controlling power.

A: The whole city lived under the Pope's power. All churches could be closed. No priest was allowed into a city until the people repented.

B: What's that power called?

A: The power of interdict.

B: The doors of the churches were locked?

A: And the bells silenced. The dead lay unburied. Such was the power.

B: More powerful than kings.

A: More power was in the national office of the Church than in Cyrus, Alexander, and Caesar.

B: Over the destiny of souls. Future. Life.

A: And the Pope kept kings kneeling and repenting in deep snow.

B: Help me see it in a rhyme.

A: The bells of the city are still,
  And dead as the church on the hill.
  The kings on their knees
  Say: Thank you, and please,
  And wait for the papal "I will."

B: Think of the good this power could have done. Think of all the life that could have been set free with that temporal and spiritual power.

A: Wars could have been stopped. Justice and peace were a fingertip away.

B: A heart away. Where did it all end up?

A: Rome became the headquarters for the power. The capital of the Holy Roman Empire was in Rome.

B: Why Rome?

A: The imperial government was already there. The statesmen, poets, orators, and philosophers were in Rome. The great armies, the wealth, the power, and the beauty was there.

B: That's when Rome went into ruins.

A: The church rose up out of the ruins.

B: Who did it?

A: The apostle Peter lived in Rome. The tradition is that he was crucified there.

B: How did Peter get the power, or give it on?

A: It came from Jesus to Peter. By the laying on of hands, he inherited the keys of Christ, to open and to close heaven.

B: And the bishops took the power from Peter.

A: The bishops explained to the people that Peter was the heir and successor to Christ. Rome was where the power was.

B: Then came the missionaries.

A: Yes. And then all the popes. And then excommunication.

B: And the power of interdict. Now it's my turn for a limerick.

> The apostle St. Peter was given
> The keys to the Kingdom of Heaven;
> The Church used Christ's grace
> To wage war and disgrace,
> And keep empires from going to heaven.

A: Isn't that going a bit too far?

B: Which, the fact or the rhyme?

Saved

Setting: Exhibit various paintings, sketches, sculptures of Christ. These may be traditional, professional, or amateur paintings from the community, chosen to show particular ways Christ is imagined to be.

A: Keep the law and you will be saved.

B: I cannot.

A: Then you will die.

B: I know. It leaves me no choice. Either I do or I die. Either or.

A: What's the alternative?

B: If I had power over sin.

A: And death.

B: I cannot, so I'm trapped.

A: There's another way to see it all.

B: How do you know?

A: In Christ, God gives another way to see reality.

B: What's the picture?

A: It's a new way of seeing the world. Luther saw it.

B: No longer the dead end: Keep the law or die.

A: It's a breakthrough, a discovery.

B: A discovery?

A: The breakthrough is that the Christian life is not the cause of salvation.

B: What then?

A: It is the fruit of salvation. Christ gives us a new way to see life. Salvation begins the new life.

B: What is the new picture?

A: It's really a new way of seeing God: There is only God. In God we live and move and have our being.

B: We are part of this new picture?

A: Even while we have need.

B: We don't have to live up to something?

A: We live out of something. We live out salvation.

B: How do we get into this picture?

A: Through God. God gives us the will to express this salvation.

B: How can we express it?

A: Through our own uniqueness. Each one is different. We create our own meaning.

B: Then it's not our own will or purpose, finally.

A: It's God's will we live. We don't have to justify it, or ourselves.

B: Or save ourselves.

A: We only express this will of God, to do the will of God.

B: Then we're not on our own, as it were, trying to please God.

A: We're never separated and alone, in isolation. We are always in relationship.

B: We're not trying to keep the law to be saved.

A: We're not autonomous, on our own, aspiring to be creators.

B: We are expressing God's will in meaningful ways. Our ways.

A: Our own meaning is connected to God's will and purpose. We cannot or need not justify ourselves, for the will we live is not our will.

B: It is God's will.

A: And that's the new picture Luther had of how things are.

B: In Christ we see the real picture. He was one with the Father.

A: We are reborn into this relationship, this intimacy with God.

B: And one another. We are always belonging.

A: It's a joyful picture. Meaningful.

B: Alive. Separation from God is death. Intimacy with God is our life.

A: Luther struggled with the question: How can life be more joyful and more gracious?

B: He said that Christ delivered him from sin, death, and the power of the devil.

A: He was looking for power over these.

B: He found it in the new picture. More gracious.

A: In Christ.

Love

Setting: The scene includes calculators, the Catechism, and a box of valentines for later distribution.

A: Why the calculator?

B: I'm trying to figure out what a thousand generations in my family looks like.

A: A thousand?

B: Thousands of generations.

A: Starting when?

B: With myself. Thousands of generations times myself. Thousands of generations times all my family and relatives.

A: Thousands of people.

B: Many thousands. I'm figuring out thousands of generations after this one, after mine.

A: What does your calculator say now?

B: I can't read it anymore. I don't think it goes that far.

A: Who gave you this idea to figure this many generations?

B: Martin Luther. He said that's how far love goes. It multiplies into thousands of generations.

A: What are you doing with the other calculator?

B: It's for calculating hate and anger. The first one shows how love multiplies. This one is for anger.

A: How far are you figuring?

B: Three or four generations times myself. I've got it all here.

A: Where did you get the idea of hate and anger going on for three or four generations?

B: From Martin Luther. He said that's how far hate travels.

A: What does that mean to you?

B: It means that love goes farther than hate. Anger wears out in three or four generations.

A: But love goes into thousands of generations.

B: If you love God and keep the commandments.

A: Where did Martin Luther find out about this?

B: From God. He found it recorded in the Bible. And God told it to Moses.

A: Love is stronger. It lives longer. Hate wears out.

B: And love overcomes hate.

A: Love is stronger and older.

B: The calculators have helped me see this again.

A: You sure can tell the difference between love and hate.

B: Hate is weaker.

A: Love is stronger. It lasts forever.

B: Charity is the greatest.

The Cross

Setting: A and B are seated beside a cross; they talk while in a contemplative mood.

A: There is something missing.

B: The other side is missing.

A: The other side?

B: Death. You can't know life unless you face death.

A: It's always going on—the underside.

B: The other side.

A: The opposite.

B: What about faith?

A: It rises out of the underside—doubt.

B: The other side of faith is doubt.

A: We pass from one to the other.

B: Back and forth.

A: From storm to peace.

B: Faith made Martin know he was strong. He knew faith in the middle of the storm.

A: He knew courage in the middle of death. The bounty was on his head.

B: Paul found his faith while on a road to Damascus.

A: Peter found faith while floundering and falling in the Sea of Galilee.

B: Martin found faith on the way to the meeting in the city of Worms. When he was most desperate, he received strength.

A: His faith was like new.

B: Faith is always like new. It was new for Sarah and Abraham. It was new for old Hannah. Now it was like new for Martin.

A: New, because he was pulled from death to life.

B: From fear to trust.

A: From being hunted to being freed.

B: From being empty to being full.

A: From being needy to having plenty. Martin was in trouble. And when he was in his depths, the Spirit of God put Martin's spirit on top. At Worms he spoke like a new man.

B: Like a person just saved—rescued and freed.

A: He had all the energy and nerve he needed to stand against the whole Church and the whole Empire.

B: God's Spirit can get into the human spirit when it needs it.

A: When you ask and beg for it—expect it.

B: And are open to it.

A: Martin was desperate. He was at point zero.

B: A bounty was on his head. People could make money by shooting him. He was posted on the "most wanted" list.

A: Dangerous.

B: A criminal.

A: A cross was waiting for him—a cross of the Church or of the state.

B: A burning stake. Death.

A: That's where God revealed himself to Martin. At the point of death.

B: God was the one on the cross.

A: The derelict on the cross.

B: Martin was on the way to the cross, and there he met Christ—on the same road.

A: Going to the cross.

B: Martin's journey to Worms was the Dolorosa—the way to the cross.

A: He recognized it.

B: When he saw the cross, he saw God.

A: And then he took heart.

B: That's when the courage came. When he saw God on the cross, Martin was no longer afraid.

A: He had courage.

B: That's when faith came. When he saw the cross.

A: The rest of the way was after the cross.

B: Down hill—over the hill—after the hill—any way you want to say it.

A: Or see it. You can get to the other side, but only from the side of the cross.

B: The two sides are connected. One leads into the other.

A: Inside the person is where they connect.

B: In slavery comes freedom.

A: When there's nowhere else to flee—it all begins.

B: That's the other side. Martin took it, and went on from there.

A: Freed, and able to stand.

Me

Setting: The readers stand before a mirror and look at themselves as they read from Martin Luther's "Small Catechism." They come across the words of the Second Article: "Who has redeemed me." They repeat these words while looking at themselves in the mirror. The drama may conclude by handing the mirror to others who repeat the words: "redeemed me."

A: He has saved and redeemed me.

B: Me.

A: A lost and condemned creature.

B: Me.

A: That's what Martin said: "Me—saved me—Martin."

B: He could have said: "us."

A: He said: "me."

B: It means something. He never wrote anything in the Catechism without meaning it. Every word was weighed.

A: Me—it's so personal.

B: Do you like the idea?

A: Who wouldn't—God thinking about me.

B: How intimate.

A: That's how Martin thought about God. He talked with God as though he was with a friend.

B: It was not a formal meeting. He learned to see God not as stuffy or distant or stern.

A: How do we know?

B: By the way he talked to God. He called God "du."

A: "Du"? What's "du"?

B: He said "du" instead of "sie." "Sie" is proper and polite. It means "you." "Sie" is what you say to dignitaries and queens and kings.

A: And "du"?

B: "Du" also means "you." "Du" is what you say to family—to your child—to your mother.

A: That's how he talked with God?

B: He said "du." He was his friend.

A: And that's why Martin could say "me"—"who has redeemed me."

B: "Me" is like "du"—they both feel like family.

A: "Du" and "me" are like each other. God and Martin were family to each other—the best of friends.

B: God has saved "me."

A: Me.

Revelation

Setting: A poncho or shawl with a bouquet of flowers will create the mood.

A: It was 1531—in Mexico—on a country road.

B: San Diego—an Indian boy—was on the dusty road.

A: It was a time in which the bishop would not build a church for the people.

B: He needed persuading. That is how the legend goes.

A: Then Mary, the mother of Jesus, appeared to the boy.

B: Not in his sleep, but while he was on the road.

A: She showed him a bush of flowers and blossoms ready for the picking.

B: It was in a season and a place where these blossoms were not to be found. The boy clutched them into his poncho as he was told to do.

A: He took them to the bishop with the word that these were a sign that the church should be built.

B: The bishop was astonished at the dream and the boy's telling of it.

A: But the boy could not convince the bishop.

B: There was one more sign in the shawl of the Indian boy. The flowers had made an imprint of Mary upon the shawl. The picture was there.

A: That's how the story went.

B: That's how the church was built. The church was named for the dream—"The Church of the Virgin of Guadalupe."

A: It was 1531.

B: A similar story was happening in Germany.

A: A peasant boy had a dream.

B: The Catechisms of Luther were now two years old.

A: The Augsburg Confession was being signed.

B: Katie and Martin had been married eight years.

A: Charles V was King of the Holy Roman Empire of Germany.

B: The same Charles V was ruler of the Mexican village of the Indian boy.

A: The king from Spain was ruler of both places.

B: Luther was the son of a miner. A bolt of lightning threw him in fear to the ground and he shouted: "St. Anne, help me, and I will become a monk."

A: St. Anne was the mother of Mary, the mother of Jesus. She was the saint of the miners.

B: Like the Indian boy, this peasant youth was receiving a message.

A: He did not go to the bishop to request that another cathedral be built in Erfurt.

B: In time, he went to all the bishops and priests and archbishops to say that the church should be rebuilt.

A: Not a building.

B: It should be renewed. God's message was not getting through to the people.

A: Neither in Mexico nor in Germany. The gospel was hidden.

B: The Indian boy wanted a church in his village.

A: The boy from Saxony wanted a new church, renewed.

B: The Indian boy found the miracle in the flowers and the shawl.

A: Martin knew of such a miracle in the German legend of Elizabeth. The miracle he saw was in the images of Christ in the Scriptures.

B: When he saw them, he hurried to show the whole hierarchy. It was a word of revelation.

A: Just as the Indian boy had hurried to his village bishop.

B: For the Indian boy it was a dream; for in Mexico, as in Germany, it was hard to see Christ.

A: One saw Christ in the sign of the bouquet and the imprint on the shawl.

B: The other saw revelation in the lightning of the storm.

A: Then in the Christ in the hay—and the God on the cross.

B: The sign may be near a burning bush.

A: Through a dream in Mexico.

B: In a storm on a German road.

History Songs

Instructions

Hymns generally carry markings that refer to their tunes and the designated meters, such as 8888, LM, 7777, SM, or 7676D. These numbers indicate the number of beats in each line. For example, 8888 means that each stanza has four lines and each line has eight beats. D indicates that the first four lines are repeated in the stanza.

The following hymn tunes are suggestions that can be used as melodies for singing the Luther History Songs. Or, if you like, substitute some other hymn tune that is more familiar or more fitting for the text. Songwriters may wish to write their own original melodies for these texts.

You can also use the History Songs, Reading Dramas, Luther Sayings, and texts from Luther's life for a Luther musical, a festival, or simply for education and inspiration.

7777 Type Songs

Hark the Herald Angels Sing
As with Gladness, Men of Old
Go to Dark Gethsemane
Rock of Ages
Jesus Saviour, Pilot Me

Spread, Oh Spread, Almighty Word
Take My Life and Let It Be
Come, Ye Thankful People, Come
For the Beauty of the Earth
Angels We Have Heard on High
Let Us with a Gladsome Voice

7676 Type Songs

When Christmas Morn Is Dawning
Rejoice, Rejoice, Believers
O Sacred Head Now Wounded
O Living Bread from Heaven
O Word of God Incarnate
Abide with Us, Our Saviour
I Lay My Sins on Jesus
The Church's One Foundation
Stand Up, Stand Up for Jesus
Lead On, O King Eternal
O, Jesus, I Have Promised

8686 and CM Type Songs

I Am So Glad
Alas, and Did My Saviour Die
There Is a Green Hill Far Away
We Praise You, Lord

This Is the Spirit's Entry Now
Almighty God, Your Word Is Cast
Father of Mercies
Jesus, the Very Thought of Thee
O God, Our Help in Ages Past
In Christ There Is No East or West
Amazing Grace
My God, How Wonderful Thou Art
Oh That the Lord Would Guide My Way
All Hail the Power of Jesus' Name
According to Thy Gracious Word
There Is a Fountain Filled with Blood

8787 Type Songs

Angels from the Realms of Glory
Jesus, Refuge of the Weary
In the Cross of Christ I Glory
Glory Be to God the Father
There's a Wideness in God's Mercy
Love Divine, All Love Excelling
Joyful, Joyful We Adore Thee

6686 or SM Type Songs

Rise Up, O Saints of God
We Give Thee but Thine Own
Great Is the Lord
Lord Jesus, Think of Me
Wide Open Are Thy Hands

8888 or LM Type Songs

Lord, Keep Us Steadfast in Thy Word
All People That on Earth Do Dwell
Lord Jesus Christ, Be Present Now
Awake, My Soul
All Praise to Thee, My God, This Night
Lord, Speak to Us
Children of the Heavenly Father
Give to Our God Immortal Praise
Eternal Father, Strong to Save
For the Beauty of the Earth

These Luther History Songs may be read aloud or sung. The meter signatures and hymn tunes provide help for singing, playing, and enjoying them in private, group, congregation, and festival use.

Ten November

Ten November, late at night,
Martin born by candlelight.
Eisleben, O little town—
Moon is out and God is down.

Margaretha, give your boy
Piety, and give him joy.
Give him heart so he may see
Christ inside the stormy sea.

Hans with infant one day old,
Through the morning autumn cold
To the fortress on the hill:
Word and water; all is still.

Priest and Hans and son—the three
Stood inside the baptistry.
There they met in Easter morn.
Baptism and child reborn.

Hymn Type: 7777
Tune: Spread, Oh Spread, Almighty Word

Latin Latin

Latin school for seven years;
Playing Latin with his peers;
Latin grammar, Latin cheers;
Latin joy and Latin tears.
Martin's faith and Martin's fears
Inside seven Latin years.

Latin only, word or deed;
Ten Commandments and the Creed.
Learn your Latin, learn to lead;
Learn to love and intercede.
Martin you will too succeed
If your Latin you will heed.

Latin takes the people far:
To the teachers' seminar;
Lawyers who will pass the bar;
Diplomats who go afar;
Scientists of sea and star.
Latin, Latin takes you far.

Hymn Type: 777777
Tune: As With Gladness

Hans

Now some have said of Father Hans,
He wasn't always kind;
Too harsh at times, his anger weighed
On Martin's tender mind.

When Martin was away from home
His father's stern discord
Was coloring the faith and thought
Of Martin to the Lord.

He wished that God would judge him less
And would all life approve,
For Martin felt the grace of God
Was hiding realms above.

Now others say that father Hans
And Martin were quite near,
For everyone in Luther's times
Felt terror and knew fear.

Hymn Type: 8686
Tune: There Is a Fountain Filled with Blood

Erfurt Erfurt

Now there goes Martin walking West
Into the setting sun,
At seventeen and at his best,
For study and for fun.

Dear Erfurt, Erfurt is the cheer,
And friends came very quick,
With lute and song and drinking beer
And talk by candlestick.

Arithmetic, astronomy,
And music in the air;
Philosophy, geometry,
With reading and with pray'r.

So Martin Luther, fill your brain
With more philosophy;
Learn law and never know again
The life of peasantry.

Hymn Type: 8686
Tune: I Am So Glad

Martin

Martin, Martin by the tree,
Wind and storm surrounding thee;
Does the lightning of the sky
Make you think that you will die?
Martin, Martin, why the plea
Crying out inside of thee?
Is there hidden deep inside
Something you will soon confide?

Martin, Martin, on your knees,
Oh the begging, oh the pleas.
Is there something God once said
That put fear inside your head?
Martin, Martin, rise and climb
From this storm in Stotternheim.
To the cloister, then the Mass.
Grace will come, the fear will pass.

Hymn Type: 7777
Tune: Come, Ye Thankful People, Come

The Friar

In work and study, dark and light
He'd set the spirit free,
For Martin now had day and night
To live theology.

His body bore a cowl of black,
A white yoke to his feet;
The weight of Christ hung on his back
And made him God's elite.

A tonsure fringe of hair was worn
Around the friar's head;
It represented crown and thorn
Of Christ when he was dead.

Oh, Father, I am full of sin,
My list is very long,
So I recite my sins again
For I have done Thee wrong.

Hymn Type: 8686
Tune: Almighty God, Your Word Is Cast Like Seed

Daily Trust

Dear Martin, you will learn
To live in daily trust;
'Tis not what you will do or earn
But grace alone is just.

In baptism you view
A lifetime, day by day.
Each night and morning all is new;
Each day is all the Way.

Obedience to grace
Will bend the spirit low.
For love and grace is God's embrace;
The emblem is the Bow.

Hymn Type: 6686
Tune: We Give Thee But Thine Own

The Terror

The terror of my heart has gone;
The Gospel I behold.
I know the Love of God I'm in,
And Christ has made me bold.

The terror of my heart is gone,
My anxious heart is sure,
The resurrection life is key;
Christ Jesus is the door.

The terror of my God is gone
And love did take its place.
In Jesus Christ my hope has come;
By faith I own the grace.

The terror of my God is gone
And death will dance no more;
Christ rids the spirit of despair,
And death will dance no more.

Hymn Type: 8686
Tune: O God Our Help in Ages Past

My God

My God, I cry out unto Thee,
I cannot find Thy love;
The swords are piercing through Thy cheeks
And demons wing above.

And if the day will ever come
That I will know Thee well,
Then show me that Thy love will save
My soul from daily hell.

And if a cross is nailed to me,
I pray Thee take me down,
And lay me in Thy holy grave
And give my life Thy crown.

This wonder that I ask of Thee,
I need along the Way.
Not when I die, but every morn;
I need love day by day.

Hymn Type: 8686
Tune: Father of Mercies

The Press

Oh, Martin Luther, can you see
What all your theses did?
For lo the Empire of a king
Has blown off its lid.

Now German people know they are
A people with a soul;
For language, culture, and the faith
Will make the nation whole.

New printing presses have been born,
All waiting in a row;
And the whole world will read your word
And see the Spirit blow.

No one could ever write by hand
What time and world must know;
It was the Lord and printing press
Made Reformation go.

While printers tighten down the press
To let the pamphlets fly,
The truth will find its voice to speak
Or know the reason why.

Hymn Type: 7676
Tune: Father of Mercies

Here I Stand

"God help me, here I stand!"
'Twas written that he said.
"I can't do otherwise. Amen!"
A bounty on his head!

The crowd gave him a cheer;
Confusion spread through all.
Some bowed their heads, some gave a shout
Inside the Diet Hall.

The verdict was a cheer.
The Church had made the charge.
The edict sounded loud and clear:
"A heretic at large!"

The Council now was done;
All heard what he had said.
A cart would carry Martin home;
The Wartburg lay ahead.

They took him by surprise,
The horsemen in the night.
The mote! The gate! The Kutcher's room!
And he was out of sight.

So many sighed and cried,
Now overcome with gloom,
For who will preach Christ crucified
If death took Martin home?

A fortress was his bed,
In forest dark and deep;
The Word was shield and mighty rock,
And angels watch did keep.

Hymn Type: 6686
Tune: Lord Jesus, Think of Thee

Inside the Castle

He faced a long and lonely time
Inside the Castle stone;
Temptation, sickness, and despair
Did try him to the bone.

By letter he did once confess
Temptation he was in:
Lust, laziness, and idleness
Submerged his mind in sin.

The Holy Spirit knew the place,
And set his heart afire;
The people must have begged for grace
For Martin grew inspired.

As Junker Georg he'd take a ride;
His hair and beard were long.
He'd ride into the countryside
And sing the people's song.

And there did pass a year of grace;
He lived in knight's disguise.
He rode to Wittenberg one day
And took them by surprise.

Old Lucas Cranach painted him
In Wittenberg one night.
The portrait name is Junker Georg,
And Martin is the knight.

Hymn Type: 8686
Tune: My God How Wonderful Thou Art

Translating

In silent Wartburg Castle
The translating began;
God's Word turned into German—
The psalms a diadem.
He read with jubilation
The joy of David's songs,
And healing and salvation
Unfolded in the psalms.

Old psalms so filled with beauty,
Of myriad pictures bright;
He saw their text and color;
The psalms gave Martin sight.
He saw the Church reflected;
He found himself inside,
While God and all creation
Through psalms now opened wide.

The psalms once only Latin
For learned souls to pray,
Were now for all the people
To pray and sing each day.
Old songs for pray'r and singing,
Now had a German look,
And through the hand of Martin
Became a prayer book.

Hymn Type: 7676
Tune: O Word of God Incarnate

The Spirit

In the fortress of the Wartburg,
Martin heard the spirits thunder;
Overhead, inside, and under
Came the wonder of the Spirit.

In the fortress of the Wartburg,
In the awesome midnight hour,
In the darkness of the tower
Came the power of the Spirit.

In the fortress of the Wartburg,
Midst the bats and demons reeling,
Inside Martin and his feeling
Came the healing of the Spirit.

In the fortress of the Wartburg,
Trees and spirit bending, blowing,
Pen and inkwell everflowing,
Came the glowing of the Spirit.

In the fortress of the Wartburg,
By the prayer and the writing,
In the holy candlelighting
Came the lighting of the Spirit.

Hymn Type: 8888
Tune: Children of the Heavenly Father

Monster

The seven-headed monster,
Pope Leo on his back,
And all the church kneels begging,
His tail a whip to crack.
The seven-headed monster,
It is so plain to see:
Then Martin becomes monster
Drawn by an enemy.

The seven-headed monster:
The anti-Christ is pope
Who holds all in their exile
And robs them of their hope.
The seven-headed monster:
The cartoon waged a war,
As Luther tried to stop them,
The artists worked the more.

Hymn Type: 7676
Tune: All Glory, Laud and Honor

Hunted

He hunted in his childhood.
He hunted with his dad.
And sorted through the thoughts he knew
When he was very sad.

He hunted on his mother's lap
And listened at her knee.
He listened to the tales she told
And to her piety.

He hunted in the thoughts of men
And hunted in his home.
He even walked across the Alps
And hunted it in Rome.

He hunted in the sacraments.
He hunted for one word.
He begged and pled and searched each thought
Of Scripture and the Lord.

He hunted in the library.
He hunted book on book.
He hunted page by page again
And took a second look.

He hunted in the solitude.
He hunted in the psalms.
He hunted inside poverty
By begging for his alms.

He hunted in hilarity.
He hunted in a storm.
Sometimes he thought that he was near.
He wasn't even warm.

He hunted in the canticles.
He hunted while he prayed.
He hunted with his counselor.
He hunted when afraid.

He hunted in the lecture halls,
In universities,
Inside cathedrals and in shrines.
He hunted on his knees.

He hunted till he gave it up,
And felt God's own embrace.
He didn't hunt a minute more.
He found the word was grace.

The word he hunted was in fact
A word he did not own,
For grace and faith belong to God
As word of God alone.

Hymn Type: 8686
Tune: Jesus, the Very Thought of Thee

Sing

Sing, children, sing;
Your silent time is o'er.
Sing your thanks and praise to God,
Sing your thanks and praise to God
And let the Spirit soar.

Sing, children, sing;
Sing in your marketplace,
Carols in your fields and homes,
Carols in your fields and homes,
Let music bear your grace.

Sing, children, sing,
With meter in your songs,
With a rhyme and rhythm sing,
With a rhyme and rhythm sing
Your Gospel and your psalms.

Sing, children, sing,
The resurrection hope,
Till the grace and work of Christ,
Till the grace and work of Christ
Be heard at work and home.

Sing, children, sing;
It is your way to teach.
Singing helps the children pray,
Singing helps the children pray
And helps the preacher preach.

Sing, children, sing,
With body and the soul.
Singing and the Gospel heal,
Singing and the Gospel heal,
To make the people whole.

Sing, children, sing,
Oh sing, for it is so:
Christ the Fortress is our God,
Christ the Fortress is our God
Who makes the Gospel go.

Hymn Type: 4686
Tune: Sleep, Baby, Sleep

Catechism

He traveled through the villages,
And Luther was appalled
To find how little faith they knew
As church on church he called.

"What misery I now have seen;
They know not how to pray.
They need a Creed, a faith to say
By heart along the way."

"They live as poor as cattle live
And senseless as the swine;
They need a book to help them pray
To take their bread and wine."

Two Catechisms he did write
For church, the home, and school;
It helped to spark the inner light
Inside the Golden Rule.

Once Katie said in simple truth
And half in ecstasy:
"The Catechism tells me all
About my God and me."

Hymn Type: 8686
Tune: In Christ There Is No East or West

All Are Equal

Everyone a serving priest,
All are equal, none is least,
Before God all are the same,
All are one in Jesus' name.

Congregation, choose the one
Who will lead you to the Son.
Town and parish, choose your priest;
All are equal, none is least.

Hymn Type: 7777D
Tune: Come, Ye Thankful People, Come

The Manse

The Manse where Doctor Luther lived
Became the Luther home;
Eleven children they did raise,
Plus six who were their own.

Twelve homeless students lodged with them,
And often it did seem
That those who made the place their home
Were like an endless stream.

The house was filled with constant sound
And full of people noise,
Of papers, books, and Table Talks,
And songs and children's toys.

Dear Katie managed all the chores;
She was indeed in charge,
And rose at four to do the work,
The household was so large.

She kept the pigs, the cows, the goats
And brewed the Luther beer,
And planted orchards, canned the fruit,
And dressed the wild deer.

When students wrote throughout the meal
Then Katie turned to scold:
"Come, Martin, eat instead of talk;
Your soup is growing cold."

And if his language sounded rough
And idioms grew coarse,
She'd tell them all to watch their tongues
Before the talk grew worse.

When Martin was again depressed,
And sometimes filled with glee,
Then Katie would in times of ill
Restore his energy.

She used the herbs as daily cures,
So common in their day:
The dung of cow was mixed with wine
To brighten up his day.

There was a joy inside the house
Of Jesus and His love;
The family was a place for God,
A foretaste of above.

By lyre and lute, by Christ and song
God heals the family,
For music is the gift of God
Next to theology.

Hymn Type: 8686
Tune: There Is a Green Hill Far Away

Katie

He traveled far to do his work,
He faced both peace and harm.
He wrote how much he missed them all;
His letters were so warm.

He teased dear Katie when he wrote,
For Katie meant a "chain."
Her name showed he was bound to her
In gladness and in pain.

He helped her when she worried much
And could not rest or sleep;
And they did give it up to God
To do and care and keep.

"Dear Katie, leave it all to God
To care for you and me,
Lest the whole earth consume us all
Inside its travesty."

Hymn Type: 8686
Tune: I Am So Glad

In God's Emblem

He traveled to Eisleben
To do what he could do
To end the war of two Counts;
And he was sixty-two.
Oh Katie was so anxious
For he was not so well;
She wrote him many letters.
He lay beneath a spell.

"Dear Katie, don't be troubled;
My God protects me here,
And more than you and angels
His peace will conquer fear.
Who lay inside a manger
And fondled maiden breast,
Now sits beside the Father
And gives your Martin rest."

And there inside Eisleben
He died in awesome night,
Where life had its beginning.
And both by candlelight.
The circle of the fountain
Encircled him with grace;
The grip of death and dancing
Were held in God's embrace.

His friends did break the message:
"Elijah has gone home:
The horseman and the chariots,
And we are left alone."
His friends retold the message:
"The soul is in the air;
Elijah is triumphant,
The mantle we will wear."

Hymn Type: 7676D
Tune: Lead On, O King Eternal

Little Town

In little town of Eisleben
'Neath trees of Saxony,
A child was born by candlelight
In fourteen-eighty-three.
To Hans and Margaretha
God sent by night a birth,
And in the child a miracle
Lay newborn on the earth.

In little church of Saint Petri
The baby one day old.
The enemy will seek the child,
The font is bitter cold.
The boy will meet all evil
With cross upon his face,
For Martin is a child of God
Wrapped up inside God's grace.

In little town of Magdeburg
A prince gave all away;
He walked the streets with empty hands,
A beggar night and day.
God's grace is for the taking
And this the great surprise:
Christ Jesus is the gift to all,
Receiving is the prize.

In little town of Eisenach
A teacher tipped his hat,
He honored children as they came
Who never forgot that
The joy of consecration
Can lift a life so high
That little children find their home:
God's mansion in the sky.

In little town of Wittenberg
His daughter in his arm—
The Lord of heaven took her home
Beyond all pain or harm.
When death comes in the morning,
When sorrow turns to pain,
We know the voice that whispers sure:
We too will meet again.

I am the child of Saxony
By water and the word.
My tempest and my stormy waves
Are silenced by the Lord.
It is God's word of mercy
That makes the storm be still,
And when Christ says, "Receive my peace."
I will. I will. I will.

How certainly, how certainly
The grace of God is true.
Amen, amen to every day.
Each morning grace is new.
First God did draw the circle,
A ring around the soul,
With hope and love inside God's ring
For Christ has made us whole.

Hymn Type: 8686, 7686
Tune: O Little Town of Bethlehem

Map of Luther's Journey

Magdeburg ●

● Halberstadt

Mansfeld ●
● Eisleben

H...

● Nordhausen

● Muhlhausen

● Eisenach

● Gotha ● Erfurt ● Weimar

Naumbu...

● Moehra

Jena ●

Gera

● Schmalkalden

Plauen

To Worms

● Coburg

Hof ●

To Heidelberg

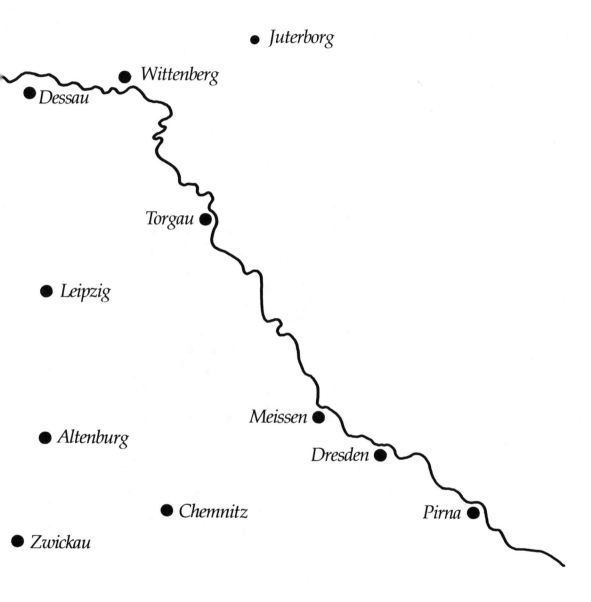

To Berlin

● Juterborg

● Wittenberg

● Dessau

Torgau ●

● Leipzig

● Altenburg

Meissen ●

Dresden ●

● Chemnitz

Pirna ●

● Zwickau

Take a Tour
Through the Pages of
A Pilgrimage to Luther's Germany

Herb Brokering
with Roland Bainton

A beautiful pictoral meditation in celebration of the 500th anniversary of Martin Luther's birth.

Combines noted historian Roland Bainton's Luther research with Brokering's festive prose and poetry. They recently collaborated in making the film *Where Luther Walked* in East Germany.

Recalling the times and places of importance in Luther's life, *A Pilgrimage to Luther's Germany* gives all Christians a better understanding of the heritage Luther set in motion. The authors capture this heritage in poignant photos of historical places and contemporary life in Germany.

This insightful book portrays Luther as a Gothic man in feudal times—a man whose legacy is alive today. Looks at how Luther viewed Christ, the family, the Church and State, and more. Deals with the Reformer's theological turmoil and resolution.

Herbert Brokering is a pastor of the American Lutheran Church as well as a poet and educator. Among his books is *Pilgrimage to Renewal*. Brokering lives in Minneapolis, Minnesota.

Roland Bainton, prince of Luther scholars, is professor emeritus at Yale Divinity School. The most famous of his thirty books is *Here I Stand: A Life of Martin Luther,* with a million copies in half a dozen languages.

Oversized format and full-color photographs throughout make this a beautiful, affordable remembrance of Luther's anniversary year.

Herr, du wirst wiederkommen.
Du wirst wiederkommen in Kraft,
und sie wird mir gehören.

Du wirst wiederkommen in Herrlichkeit,
und du wirst sie mir offenbaren.
Du wirst abwischen alle Tränen
und meine Traurigkeit wird ein Ende nehmen.

Du wirst den Tod auslöschen,
und ich werde leben für immer.
Du wirst wiederkommen,
und ich werde dich sehen, wie du bist.

Du wirst zu mir sagen: „Ich bin's",
und ich werde wissen,
daß es deine Worte waren.
Du wirst wiederkommen,
und ich werde leben.

Wenn du wiederkommst,
so komm in Macht und Herrlichkeit, Jesus.

Herbert F. Brokering

From Gebete (Gutersloh Verlaghaus/Gerd Mohn), the German edition of Surprise Me, Jesus by Herbert Brokering © 1974 Augsburg Publishing House, 422 South Fifth Street, Minneapolis, Mn. 55440.

Also from HERB BROKERING . . .

Three more books to help you celebrate your Christian faith!

Wholly Holy explores the freshness, the joy, the enthusiasm that takes place in learning. A must for anyone interested in the creative side of Christian education. $4.95

Love Songs: Musical Activities for Christian Education and *Joy Songs* each include the lyrics and musical accompaniment to fourteen songs by Herb and Lois Brokering. With each song is a text that provides ideas for using the songs in both educational and festive settings. $4.95

Order from: Brokering Press, 11641 Palmer Rd., Bloomington, MN 55437

Please send me copies of the books indicated below. Enclosed is $_____

____Copies of *Wholly Holy* @ $4.95 each . . $_____

____Copies of *Love Songs* @ $4.95 each . . $_____

____Copies of *Joy Songs* @ $4.95 each . . . $_____

Shipping and handling: 50¢ per copy . . . $_____

                              TOTAL . . . . . . $_____

Name_____

Address_____

_____Zip_____

Please send me copies of the books indicated below. Enclosed is $_____

____Copies of *Wholly Holy* @ $4.95 each . . $_____

____Copies of *Love Songs* @ $4.95 each . . $_____

____Copies of *Joy Songs* @ $4.95 each . . . $_____

Shipping and handling: 50¢ per copy . . . $_____

                              TOTAL . . . . . . $_____

Name_____

Address_____

_____Zip_____

Lord,
there's snow upon my feet;
the walking's slick on frozen sleet,
So pick me up if I fall down
and break my soul and break my crown.

Lord,
I'm walking on some eggs;
I'm shaking hard inside my legs.
So pick me up if I fall down
and break my soul and break my crown.

Lord,
I'm falling on my knees,
stumbling over stumps and trees.
So pick me up if I fall down
and break my soul and break my crown.

Lord,
I'm back again upon the road,
have a grip upon the load.
So pick me up if I fall down
and break my soul and break my crown,

Lord,
I'm walking right along;
thank You for the trees and song.
So pick me up if I fall down
and break my soul and break my crown.

From Lord, I Want To Celebrate by Herbert Brokering © 1980 Concordia Publishing House, St. Louis, Mo.